Your Soul's LOVE

LIVING THE LOVE YOU PLANNED
BEFORE YOU WERE BORN

ROBERT SCHWARTZ

Whispering
Winds
Press

Wilmington, Ohio

ISBN: 978-0-578-75492-5 (soft cover)
ISBN: 978-0-578-87016-8 (epub)
Library of Congress Control Number: 2021904287

Printed and bound in the U.S.A.

11 10 9 8 7 6 5 4 3 2 1

Quantity discounts are available on bulk purchases of this book.
Please contact the publisher at:
Whispering Winds Press
www.yoursoulsplan.com
e-mail: rob.schwartz@yoursoulsplan.com

Cover Design by Barbara Hodge
Interior Book Design by Sara Blum

Other Books
by Robert Schwartz

*Your Soul's Plan: Discovering the Real Meaning
of the Life You Planned Before You Were Born*

*Your Soul's Gift: The Healing Power of the Life
You Planned Before You Were Born*

A Note to Readers

THERE ARE MANY PEOPLE WHO truly cannot afford to buy books. My mission is to make the healing information in this book available to as many people as possible, including those who cannot afford to purchase it. Please ask your local library to carry this book (as well as the two books listed on the previous page), or after you finish reading it, please consider donating your copy to your library. This simple act of kindness will touch many lives.

Thank you for helping me to bring a healing awareness of pre-birth planning to the world.

With gratitude,
Robert Schwartz
rob.schwartz@yoursoulsplan.com

Would You Like to Know Your Life Plans?

ROBERT SCHWARTZ IS A HYPNOTIST who offers between lives regressions. In this form of hypnosis, you yourself can talk directly with very wise, loving, and entirely nonjudgmental beings who can tell you what you planned before you were born and why, how you're doing in terms of fulfilling your plans, and how you may better fulfill your plans. These sessions are invaluable in assisting you to know the deeper purpose of your life: what your experiences mean; why certain patterns reoccur; why certain people are in your life; and what you sought prior to birth to learn from those relationships. Physical and emotional healing, forgiveness, greater peace and happiness, and a profound knowing of who you are and why you are here can come from these sessions.

For more information please visit Robert's website at www.yoursoulsplan.com or write to him directly at rob.schwartz@yoursoulsplan.com.

Dedicated to

Liesel,
my loving and beloved soulmate

and

The nonphysical team without whom
this book would not be possible

and

Tricia
Ryan
Alexa, Jorge, & Luca
Cathy
Sarah and Jim

and

Their loved ones

The world is full of magic things,
patiently waiting for our senses to grow sharper.

—W.B. Yeats

Contents

Acknowledgments

I AM DEEPLY GRATEFUL TO the courageous souls whose stories appear in this book. Motivated by love and a desire to be of service, they opened their hearts to me so that you, dear reader, may more fully open your heart to both your loved ones and yourself.

To Barbara Brodsky and Aaron, Pamela Kribbe and Jeshua, Corbie Mitleid, and Staci Wells and her spirit guide: Thank you once again for sharing your love and wisdom with the world. Truly, you are wayshowers. Traveling this road with you has been my joyful honor.

To Liesel, the love of my life: Thank you for your love and unwavering support. You inspire me each and every day to become a better version of myself.

Thank you to Sue Mann for your always insightful, incisive editing. This book could not have been in more capable hands. Thank you Emily Han for your eagle-eyed proofreading and Sara Blum for your beautiful interior layout. Thank you to Barbara Hodge for your exquisite cover design.

Thank you to Sylvia Hayse for helping to carry my books around the world.

Thank you to Dr. Linda Backman for permission to quote from the inductions you created and that I used with the people who share their stories in these pages.

This book would not have been possible without the contributions of many others who shared their wisdom and offered their support. In particular I thank Michelle McCann and Kat Baillie.

Thank you to the many guides, teachers, helpers, angels, masters, and other nonphysical beings who made this book possible, including the Beings of Light channeled by my wife. You are my teachers, teammates, and friends.

Preface

YEARS AGO WHEN I WAS forty, my life was profoundly unfulfilling. I found the corporate work I was doing to be bland and devoid of any deeper meaning. Although I longed for a romantic relationship, I was unable to manifest one. I was drifting through life seemingly rudderless, going through the motions, each new day as empty and uninspiring as the previous. I wondered why I was here on Earth. I had no idea of either the answer to that question or how to find it. At times I wished I could go Home.

In my search for meaning, I had my first session ever with a psychic medium. She channeled my spirit guides, who told me I had planned my greatest challenges for the purpose of spiritual growth *before* I was born. Shortly thereafter I met a woman who is able to channel her own soul. In some fifteen hours of channeling, her soul told me in detail how the pre-birth planning process works. The resonance I felt with the concept of pre-birth planning was clear, strong, and undeniable.

At about the same time, I had what is known as a spiritually transformative experience. One day, as I was doing nothing more than walking down the street, I felt pure, overwhelming, unconditional love for every person I saw. This love was fundamentally different from the love one might feel for a parent, child, or romantic partner; it was a divine, transcendent, all-encompassing, totally immersive, limitless love. I understood intuitively that this experience was a gift from my soul saying to me, "This love is who you really are."

I decided to leave the corporate world and write books about why we plan our biggest challenges before coming into body. In the years that followed, I wrote *Your Soul's Plan, Your Soul's Gift*, and the book you are now reading. The life that has emerged from the writing of these books is so deeply fulfilling and uniquely "me" that it would have been beyond my wildest imagination or ability to comprehend when I was forty. Equally important, the research I did for the books taught me that human suffering is not random, arbitrary, or purposeless; rather, it is rich with meaning. That understanding created a deep healing for me. My hope and intention are that it creates a similar healing for you.

It is important to understand there is not just one truncated, linear, concretized life plan—a Plan A so to speak—for each person's life. There is a Plan A, but there is also a Plan B, C, D, E, and on and on . . . so many plans that full comprehension is beyond the capacity of the human brain. These additional plans are the soul's accounting for the many and various free will choices that can be made by the incarnate human. Each of us has free will, and it is our free will that makes the Earth school a truly meaningful experience. Without free will we would be nothing more than automatons, in which case no true learning would occur or even be possible.

Plan A is the highest vibrational plan; that is, a life in which the personality (a portion of the soul's energy in a physical body) makes the most loving decisions possible in each moment. In this case there is no vibrational difference between the personality and the soul. In essence, the soul is fully inhabiting the body and living that lifetime without the dilution or alteration created by the ego or smaller self. Saints and masters may execute this plan, but the rest of us will invariably make at least some and usually many unloving decisions. Although unloving decisions can cause pain for self and others, they also result—if we live life consciously—in healing, expansion, and a greatly enhanced capacity to love. It is for this reason that making mistakes is not a "bad" thing. In fact, we came here to do just that. Our mistakes *are* our growth, and our growth *is* our service to the world and our fellow humans.

Presence and acceptance/gratitude is the divine combination that allows us to enact our higher vibrational pre-birth plans. When you are fully present to and grateful for or at least accepting of whatever arises in your experience, you tap into the Universe's field of infinite potentiality. That is, your presence and acceptance/gratitude give the Universe an energetic Yes!: a yes to healing; a yes to deeper understanding; a yes to guidance, abundance, health, spiritual clarity, and creative solutions for the highest good of all.

Giving that energetic Yes! to life requires faith and trust in the goodness of life and the Universe. We can cultivate faith and trust in several ways; one of the most important and helpful is through a *felt knowing* that the challenges we planned before birth are rich with meaning and purpose. Ultimately, this book is intended to be a pathway to that felt knowing.

Those of you who receive my email newsletter (which I invite you to sign up for at www.yoursoulsplan.com) know I have been publishing channelings done by my wife, Liesel. She channels a collective of wise, loving, deeply caring, nonphysical beings who are in a state of unity consciousness and whom we affectionately call the Beings of Light. They said the following to me about pre-birth plans:

> We are enamored of bringing together the practice of present moment awareness with your work.
>
> When viewed from a mental level, these things can seem contradictory; however, they are not necessarily so. The way in which presence (which is being present in the now moment *and* in a state of acceptance of, or gratitude for, what 'is' in the now moment) plays out in pre-birth planning is that it allows the highest version of the pre-birth plans to become the working version.
>
> We have described previously that to put our language into the English language is like trying to take an infinite number of words and distill it into some hundred words. Similarly, pre-birth planning contains within it an essentially infinite number of permutations of actual plans. This can seem contradictory to the human mind—as though this is not planning at all if there are an infinite number of possibilities—but We assure you that

this is still a kind of planning.

The plans themselves all fall under what We refer to as a probabilistic, multidimensional curve form. For purposes of visualization, a simplified version of what We mean by a multidimensional curve form is that which is shown to you within mathematics and statistics as a bell curve.

There are pre-birth plans that are very likely courses of events, and there are pre-birth plans that are on the far fringes of the bell curve. For many individuals, presence and truly deep connection with their souls may be on the far fringes of the bell curve of possibility; however, this would indeed be the highest alignment pre-birth plan that could be chosen in any given moment.

So, within the bell curve of possibilities there are pre-birth plan choices that could be made that make the Universe 'sing' more than other choices. All choices ultimately lead to learning and enlightenment, but some paths are far less circuitous than others.

The paths that are chosen that are in greatest alignment with the deepest Self, with Presence and Spirit and Consciousness, are those paths that are most direct and therefore least circuitous.

In other words, the vast majority of what is planned is set up as a possibility or probability, not a certainty. Life plans are fluid, fractal, and organic. Whether or not a particular plan actualizes depends upon the free-will decisions of the individual, the vibration of the individual in the current now moment, and the external events/free will decisions made by seemingly separate "others." To the extent one is fully present, the highest vibrational plan naturally emerges and can be actualized on the Earth plane. This version of the life plan is the least arduous and painful path to both self-realization and profound service as well as deep joy and fulfillment.

This book is the third in a series that examines the pre-birth planning of major life challenges. In the pages ahead we will look at the soul-level planning of challenges that occur in, and also in the absence of, romantic relationships. As with my previous two books, healing insight and enlightening information are gleaned from talking with wise, compassionate, nonphysical beings through mediums and channels. Barbara Brodksy channels Aaron (an ascended master) as well as The Divine Mother, a blending of the highest feminine consciousnesses (Mother Mary, Quan Yin, and others) in our universe. Corbie Mitleid channels a person's soul or higher self. Staci Wells channels her spirit guide. Pamela Kribbe channels Jesus, who uses his given Hebrew name, Jeshua.

Much additional wisdom is derived from past life regression and from Between Lives Soul Regression or BLSR, the form of hypnosis in which I specialize. In this form one can speak directly with very highly evolved nonphysical beings (often referred to as the Council of Elders) who know what was planned for the current lifetime and why, how one is doing in terms of fulfilling one's plans, and how one may better fulfill one's plans. A BLSR contains an abbreviated past life regression.

May you see yourself and your life reflected in the pages ahead. May the wisdom and healing found by these courageous souls become your wisdom and healing.

☙❧

CHAPTER 1

Infidelity

S
URVEYS INDICATE THAT ALMOST ONE in every
five adults in monogamous relationships has cheated on the
partner. Nearly half of all people admit to being unfaithful
at some point in their lives. If discovered, infidelity can destroy
trust and breed suspicion, confusion, rage, and feelings of betrayal
and perhaps inadequacy. The unfaithful partner may be racked
with guilt and even self-loathing. Bonds of love that took years to
grow can dissolve overnight.

Given the prevalence of infidelity, to me it seems likely it is
often planned before birth. Yet, why would any soul want to be
betrayed? Why would another soul agree to be the betrayer? How
can evolution be served by such a painful experience? And how
can an understanding of one's pre-birth plan be used to foster
healing in the wake of the devastation created by infidelity? To
explore these and other questions, I spoke with Tricia about the
betrayal she experienced in her marriage.

Tricia

Seventy years old at the time of our conversation, Tricia began
by telling me how she and Bob, her now-deceased husband,
had connected on their first date when both were in their early
thirties.

"We just couldn't stop finding out about each other," she recalled. "The restaurant where we had dinner closed, so we walked and walked and talked and laughed until the middle of the night. It was like I found home. This man—his exuberance and his light-heartedness! We were looking at the stars, and he asked if he could kiss me. Of course, my goodness I said 'Yes.' My knees buckled! I felt faint. I had never felt anything like it. It was this feeling of *I know this person*. After that first date, we were together." Tricia and Bob married four months later.

"Nothing bothered us," Tricia told me. "On our honeymoon in Hawaii somebody stole all our money out of our room, and we just laughed about it."

For the next seventeen years Tricia and Bob enjoyed marital harmony. The relationship was everything Tricia had ever hoped for and more. Then, abruptly, something changed.

"Bob came home from a conference, and he was telling me about this woman, Claire, he had met. I had heard her name from some of his colleagues and that she was this beautiful, young, athletic, single girl. Bob was all delighted because he had gotten a note from Claire. I said, 'Why would Claire write you a note?' He snapped at me—he'd never done that before—said 'I don't know,' jumped up off the couch and stomped away.

"There were many other hints, and one of them was very blatant. His clothing was soiled from an ejaculation. In my innocence and love for him, I remember doing the wash and thinking, 'I hope he's OK. I won't say anything because I don't want to embarrass him.' That's how naïve I was."

Tricia began having a recurring nightmare in which Bob was with Claire. In the dream he told Tricia, "I'm leaving. I don't love you anymore. I love her." When Tricia told Bob about the dream, he said, "I'm so sorry you're going through that," but he did not say there was no reason for it.

"There was one time when Bob came home from one of these meetings where Claire was a participant, and he reached to kiss me. He smelled like perfume. I backed up and said, 'That's disgusting! What is it?' He made up a story about having gone out to dinner with friends and the waitress hugging him."

Not long thereafter, Bob, who was unhappy in his job, told Tricia that he'd like to move to Oregon. She agreed. After the move he found a new job that was to his liking. Ten years passed, years in which "we recaptured the fairy tale," as Tricia put it. During this time period the troubling hints were seemingly forgotten.

Then one evening Bob was writing in his journal while Tricia prepared for bed. "I felt this flush of emotion come over me," Tricia said. "It was from my gut. I started breathing heavy. Bob said, 'Are you OK?' I said, 'No, I'm not!' The voice coming out of me was very unlike my own. I said, 'I'm feeling so much anger. I need you to do something for me. I want you to tell me everything you did with Claire.' Now, this was ten years later. We hadn't even discussed Claire; she was long gone. I had no idea why I was saying this. It was like being in a play where you have to say certain words. Bob's eyes popped! He dropped his journal, looked stricken, and said, 'We kissed a little.' I threw the phone at him and hit him in the face."

Bob then admitted that he had a year-long affair with Claire. "I fell to the floor," Tricia continued. "*I thought I would die!* We went on with this conversation through the whole night. I was so sick that I was throwing up. I was yelling words I had never used in my life. I could see the impact on his face. I heard a voice in my mind that said, 'Hold him. Just love him,' but I ignored it. Bob dissolved in regret and remorse."

Tricia yelled at Bob night after night, week after week. "Tricia, what do you want from me?" he would ask her. "I want you to die!" she would shout in response.

Six months later Bob started to feel unwell. A biopsy showed that he had the most aggressive form of prostate cancer. He was given three months to live.

Putting aside her anger, Tricia moved a hospice bed into the living room so Bob could watch TV and look at birds through the window. She slept on a pad at the foot of his bed. "I did everything for him—cared for him, bathed him, tried to get him to eat." They looked at old photos, watched movies, and talked about the happiest times in their relationship. They also found a way to heal.

"We went back in our memory and changed things to the way we hoped they would have been. We said to each other what should have been said then. We pretended that Bob had just come home from work. He'd then tell me that he had been tempted by this girl. We actually had the conversation that would have saved us at the time. It was like redoing the mistakes. It was so powerful because each time we did that it took away the sting." Gradually, subtly, Tricia felt her anger dissolving.

"I told Bob—and I was telling the truth—that I had found complete forgiveness. And I saw in him something I had never seen elsewhere in my life—unconditional love, absolute unconditional love, for me."

Then, three months after his diagnosis, Bob died.

"He lives in my heart," Tricia said softly. "I know he's there. I hear him. Sometimes I hear his voice. Sometimes it's just a feeling."

Prior to this conversation, Tricia had said she believes Bob's affair with Claire was planned by all of them before this lifetime began.

"Tricia," I asked, "what is your understanding of why each of you wanted to have this experience?"

"Bob felt—he mentioned it—that this lifetime was for him to stand up for himself and say *no* when he should, to not be manipulated by another person," she explained. I wondered if Bob now felt that he had failed in this lesson. Would he plan another lifetime to "get it right"?

"For myself," Tricia said, "I came here to learn unconditional love. Bob was my greatest teacher. Through him I learned what unconditional love is. When I was young, I stomped on hearts. I would break up with men, or I would have an affair—and once with a married man. I didn't understand the pain I was causing. The greatest lesson was to learn the cruelties that can happen when you do something without thinking of others.

"For Claire, I actually spoke to her several times. She said she felt a victim to life and that the only way she could not be a victim was to seduce people—men and women, family members—into doing her bidding, which would make her feel confident and powerful. She probably came here wanting to overcome the feeling that the world is against her. When we first spoke, I don't think she had overcome that yet. I last talked to her a few years ago; she was much wiser and was very kind to me.

"The healing that has come through this—I don't know how to explain how powerful this is because it changed all our lives."

"Tricia, some people who read this chapter will have been hurt by a partner who had an affair. They may be in the most acute part of the pain. They could read your words and think, 'It sounds like she's saying it's OK my partner cheated on me because we planned it, but I don't feel that way. I'm in agony! I'm furious!' What would you say to them?"

"When I was in the midst of all this," Tricia replied, "I don't know if there was anything that could have convinced me this was not the most horrible, tragic thing ever. If it were a movie, it would be a tragedy—but the ending would be transformational."

Tricia's comment echoed what I had seen in my clients who had healed from their greatest challenges. In the middle of the experience, it's important and necessary to acknowledge, honor, and fully feel one's pain. Years later, those who had the courage to do so spoke of how vital the life challenge had been in their evolution.

Tricia then surprised me with this revelation: Bob had once told her that the possibility of an affair with Claire had been planned by all of them before they were born.

"When did he say that?" I asked.

"In his hospice bed, a few days before his passing."

"How did he come to that awareness?"

"He would go to what he called 'the other side.' When he would come back, his eyes would shine and he would say he was told we plan our lives, that we write a script to face things to grow spiritually but that we have free will in how we respond."

I asked Tricia if there was anything else she'd like to say to someone who's in pain because the partner has had an affair.

"I know just how that person feels. What I said to myself the whole time—the words were comforting—was that he didn't do it because he doesn't love me. It had only to do with his own weaknesses, not because he doesn't love me, not because he's trying to hurt me, not because he's not a good person. Realize that you're still the same person your partner loves, and your partner is still the same person you love."

Tricia's Past Life Soul Regression

To determine if Tricia, Bob, and Claire had planned Bob's extramarital affair before they were born, Tricia and I began with a Past Life Soul Regression. I guided Tricia through the usual relaxation steps, then down a stairway and into the Hall of Records. She moved slowly along the hallway until a particular door captured her attention. I prompted her to step through the doorway and into the past life that lay behind it.

"Are you outside or inside?" I asked.

"Inside. It's a café with chairs and round tables, spacious, with counters and people behind the counters. It's day. There's light coming through the window. I'm alone. It's stuffy, warm. It smells rank—cigarette smoke.

"I have high heels on. They're plain, not terribly attractive. I'm wearing nylon stockings, a skirt—I can feel the hemline—and a brownish woman's jacket with a very bright red blouse. They're nice daytime work clothes. The skirt matches the jacket. I have fingernail polish on, a bracelet on my right arm, and a ring on my left hand. It's a gold band with another ring beside it—looks like a small stone chip—very small."

I asked Tricia to visualize a mirror in front of her face. "What do you notice about your reflection?"

"I'm a young woman, very attractive, red lipstick. I have a hat on. I have shoulder-length dark wavy hair and very light skin. I'm small and slim."

"Allow the mirror to dissolve," I said gently. "What are you doing right now?"

"I'm looking at the tables. I feel very emotional, nervous, unhappy, scared. Somebody's gonna be there. I'm meeting them. I have a purse on my right arm. I'm opening it to get a handkerchief. Occasionally people walk by the window. A man with a hat walks by. There's a newspaper on the counter. I'm walking very slowly, stopping, looking—I'm nervous. There's a room divider, a lady sitting on a high stool, a little farther two men drinking something.

"It's very quiet. A man is walking up to the door."

"Is he the person you're meeting?"

"No."

"Does the person you're meeting ever show up?"

Tricia was quiet as she allowed the scene to progress.

"No."

"How do you feel when this person doesn't show up?"

"Horrible!" she replied, pain in her voice. "Betrayed. Abandoned. Very sad. Very sad."

"Do you know who you were going to meet?"

"Somebody very important to me." She began to cry. "It's . . . my husband. This was his way of telling me that if he didn't come, he wouldn't be back. I know it now. I know it now. I am sure of it. *I hoped so, so much.*"

"Tricia, I want you to sense the energy of the man who didn't show up. Is your husband in that lifetime someone who is or was in your current life?"

"Yes," she said, her voice quivering. "It was Bob. My Bob." She started to sob.

"Allow any emotion that comes up to flow through you, knowing that tears are healing and cleansing to your soul," I suggested.

We paused for a few moments as the tears flowed. When Tricia's crying subsided, I advanced her to the next scene in that lifetime.

"There's a sidewalk, trees—beautiful, almost park-like," she described, now suddenly cheerful, "a very nice day. I'm walking, feeling happy, breathing the air. There's a young boy on a bicycle ahead of me. I wave at the boy. I know him. He's my child."

I asked if she knew whether the boy's father is the same man who had not shown up at the café.

"He's not the same man," she said with certainty. "It's a very different feeling." Often, people have such *feeling-knowing* of certain facts in their regression. It's the same type of knowing we experience when not in body and Home is on the other side.

"I'm young and healthy," she continued. "I feel like I'm maybe thirty. I'm married to the boy's father. Now I'm hugging the boy. Then he gets back on his bike. He's ahead of me now. There's a dog running in the grass. There's a building up ahead that I'm walking toward a big brick building, like an office or college building. I feel very contented, very happy, happy to be with the boy.

"I'm going into the building. I'm meeting my husband. I walk through the doors. Double doors—big, gold, very large handles. The floor inside is polished tile. The boy leaves his bicycle outside and comes with me. I hold his hand. We're walking in a hallway. There's a man"—she was now laughing joyfully—"my husband. The boy runs into his arms. I feel very happy.

"My husband is holding my waist. He's grabbing a jacket, putting it on. Now we're walking down the hall. He's holding my hand. We go out the door, and my son gets his bike. We walk back down the path I came up."

"Tricia," I said, "let's trust that your guides and soul have brought you to this scene for a reason. What do you need to know about the scene you're being shown?"

"I feel so blessed. Something very bad happened, and I got through it. That's why I feel so blessed."

"Is the bad thing that happened was that your first husband left you?"

"Yes." With this Tricia began to cry again. "I'm sure."

"Is there more for you to experience here, or are you ready to move ahead?"

"I'm ready."

"On the count of three," I instructed, "you will automatically move forward to the next significant scene or event in the life you are now experiencing. *One . . . two . . . and three!* Where are you are now, and what is happening?"

"I'm quite old now, at least sixty. I'm in my house in my bedroom. I'm alone. I feel tired and weak. I'm cold, but I can't pull the blanket over me. I can't move. My eyes are closed."

I asked Tricia if she knew whether this was the last day of that lifetime.

"I believe so."

"Do you feel complete with this scene or is there more for you to experience here?"

"I feel very complete with that life. I'm ready to move on."

"Whenever you are ready," I said, "let the life you have been examining come to a close. Your soul knows exactly what happens at the ending of a life. Your soul knows how to exit out of a physical body when a life has been completed.

"You have just died and are moving away from the physical body. You have been through this experience many times before, and you feel no physical pain or discomfort. As you move out of the body, you will be able to continue to talk to me and answer my questions because you are now in touch with your inner, true self—your soul. Feel your mind expanding into the highest levels of your being.

"We are now going to a place of expanded awareness as you move upward into the loving realm of an all-knowing, spiritual power. Even though you are only at the gateway to this beautiful realm, your soul can feel the joy at being released. Everything will become very familiar to you as we progress further, because this peaceful realm embodies an all-knowing acceptance. Now, as I count to three out loud, I want you to silently ask your spirit guide to appear when I reach the count of three. *One . . . two . . . three!* Describe the look and/or feel of your guide."

"A beautiful light," Tricia observed, a note of awe in her voice. "A woman—feels very feminine and light."

"Ask your guide to give you a name to call her."

"Reeding."

"Ask Reeding why you were shown that particular past life and what is important for you to understand about it."

Tricia then relayed to me the conversation that unfolded in her mind as I prompted her to ask a series of questions.

Reeding:	You took things too seriously in that lifetime. You found great joy when you let go.
Tricia:	What was my plan with Bob and Claire in my current lifetime? Why did we create that plan?
Reeding:	You were to know and experience unconditional love.
Tricia:	Who was I to feel it for?
Reeding:	Bob.
Tricia:	Did Bob agree to play the role he played to give me the opportunity to know unconditional love?
Reeding:	Most definitely.
Tricia:	How am I doing with learning this lesson?
Reeding:	Splendidly, though you still take yourself too seriously. Do not be afraid you will backtrack.
Tricia:	Are there other reasons I planned to experience betrayal by Bob?
Reeding:	Forgiveness.
Tricia:	In the past life I saw, did I die without having completely forgiven my first husband [Bob]?
Reeding:	Yes.
Tricia:	What else can I do to come to a place in my current lifetime of complete forgiveness and unconditional love?

Reeding: Stop resisting who you truly are. The jealousy you still feel brings guilt. The guilt makes you unaccepting of your true self, your true nature.

Tricia: How can I release the jealousy and guilt?

Reeding: You've taken it too seriously. Learn from Bob, who was a teacher of lightheartedness. You came here [to Earth] with a playful heart. You came here to play. You came here to be happy. You allowed yourself to believe that was not right. You allowed yourself to believe that was not the real you. This is a learned behavior.

Tricia: How can I unlearn this?

Reeding: Remember how to play. Remember who you were as a child. Bob came to teach you that. He was a teacher of playfulness. Remember how much fun it can be to play.

Tricia: I want to know if Bob is OK, if he loves me where he is, if he's happy, and if he loves me like he did when he was here.

Reeding: He's doing very well . . . and he adores you.

Tricia: When will I see him? Am I doing the right things in this life to be ready to be with him?

Reeding: Bob wants you to live life and to be alive while alive. You will see him again. You will be with him. And yes, he wants that, too.

With this Tricia told me that she felt complete in talking with Reeding. I began the process of bringing her out of trance: "We ask that all vows and promises tied to the past life we just examined that no longer serve be released and nullified."

"Tricia, I would like you to place in your conscious memory all that you have seen and experienced. All the thoughts, feelings, and awareness that you have gained today will continue to be useful and empower you in your current life, both consciously and unconsciously. You will now gain a sense of renewed energy and purpose. Allow this all-knowing knowledge to settle calmly within your conscious mind in proper perspective.

"As I count slowly from one to ten, I'd like you to come back into the room today with your eyes open, feeling awake and alert and able to continue to process this experience. The healing, understanding, and good work you have accomplished today will remain etched in your super-conscious mind and will be reflected in your choices, actions, and self-concept from this day forward." I then counted slowly from one to ten, increasing the volume and firmness of my voice with each count.

"Tricia, take a moment now to stretch, orient, and ground yourself. When you're ready to discuss the experience, let me know."

We sat in silence for a few moments.

"Oh, my goodness!" she suddenly announced. "It was very emotional and releasing. I feel much lighter," she said with a laugh. "And I was so struck by the woman I was looking at in the mirror—how much resemblance there was to myself as a young woman!"

I asked Tricia what she gained most from the experience.

"Number one was Bob. In the last part when I was talking with Reeding, I felt Bob so strongly and so lovingly. That was the absolute, healing part."

"What else do you feel came from this session?"

"When I experienced being stood up, it felt very familiar to me—the same anger and hurt I felt when I found that Bob had chosen that relationship with Claire."

Tricia's pre-birth plan with Bob and Claire had thus allowed her to recreate the same feelings of abandonment and betrayal that she had not been able to heal in the past life. As souls we often choose to relive a particular experience or emotion in order to master it in the current lifetime.

"Also," Tricia continued, "I saw how hard I am on myself. I've been wearing a hair shirt, so to speak. I'm hard on myself when it does nothing but harm. I saw so much good humor from Reeding. I didn't expect that at all. It feels like being forgiven by God.

"I feel like I've been given permission from the ethers—maybe self-permission—to be happy."

Tricia's Between Lives Soul Regression

Tricia's Past Life Soul Regression had given us some insight into the plan for her current lifetime. To gain greater insight, Tricia and I did a Between Lives Soul Regression (BLSR). A BLSR contains an abbreviated past life regression, but that portion of Tricia's BLSR is not relevant to the topic of infidelity and so has been omitted here.

After I guided Tricia through the initial parts of the regression, she described what she experienced as her consciousness returned to her nonphysical Home.

"I see an opening ahead of me," she began. "It's light blue. I move through it and am in an open space. There are three beings at a table. They're dressed in something that looks like translucent gowns. There's a light coming from their bodies. They have hoods over their heads.

"One of them is getting up. It's a man. He is walking toward me. He's very beautiful: sleek, soft skin, large blue eyes. He's human but doesn't look quite human. He walks over to me. He's holding my hand, looking at me."

"How does it feel to be in his presence?"

"Pure, pure love." She sounded blissful.

"Ask him if he has a name we should use."

"Milton."

"Tricia, I'd like you to ask Milton if he has any particular message for you."

"All I feel is love. I don't hear words. I just get feelings."

"I'd like you to ask Milton if we may question him and the other beings there."

"He says yes. He's walking me to the table with the others. The others are rising. There are white chairs around the table. The table is also white. I can see the other two beings now. They look very much like him, only one is female. The other is male. They're telling me their names. The female is Entera, and the other is Jonah. Jonah is walking away. I don't know why. Milton is offering me a chair. Entera is on the other side. We're sitting now."

I prompted Tricia to ask if Milton and Entera are her Council of Elders.

"Milton says they're only part of the Council. There are nine others. They are present, but I don't see them. Now Milton is putting his hands on the table. Entera puts her hands on his, and my hands are on top of theirs. Milton explains that this bonds us for conversation and makes conversation clearer so I can understand."

"Tricia, ask Milton, Entera, and the rest of your Council why you came to Earth in your current lifetime. What did you hope to accomplish?"

"Milton says that I very much wanted to address abandonment, and that it was agreed—*Oh! Bob is here! Bob is here! Bob is here!*" she announced excitedly. "Bob is walking up to me with Jonah." She began to cry softly. "Bob is dressed just like they are. He puts his hands on mine, and I smile. He sits at a chair on the opposite side. He's so full of love. There are other beings walking with Jonah to the table. I feel overcome."

I then prompted Tricia to question Bob and the Council. She relayed to me the responses she heard.

Bob: [to Tricia]	We planned this life together. I told you it would be very hard for you, but I wanted to do that [play that role] for you.
Tricia:	Why are you here with these others?
Bob:	I am with them because you're here. They help me to explain. They help you understand.

Tricia:	What was my pre-birth plan with you?
Bob:	I had things I wanted to address in this lifetime, a weakness I wanted to overcome. You wanted to help me with that. My weakness is being a pleaser. I wanted to know how to be who I really am and not be fearful. Being a pleaser is based on fear. We agreed that my choice [the affair] would help your abandonment issue, which is also an issue of fear.
Tricia:	How was I helping you to overcome the fear that made you a pleaser?
Bob:	Previously I chose lives of being dominated by others, mostly women. Also, I had a lifetime as a woman who was dominated by her world. My soul had a scar from that. In our plan you would not dominate me. You would be loving and allowing. This would allow me to see who I truly am.
Tricia:	Do you feel that was accomplished?
Bob:	Yes. Yes, I do. I'm very grateful to you.
Tricia:	Did you, Claire, and I plan the affair to give me an opportunity to learn about and rise above abandonment?
Bob:	Yes. Claire is deeply loving and is a part of the agreement out of that love. In the planning, you insisted you would be able to forgive. You, the Council, and I hoped there would be an immediate bonding and healing that would occur much earlier than it did. I hoped I would be immediately forthcoming [about the affair] and that we would heal at that moment. It didn't happen. I was too weak, and so it went on and on.

Entera: There was a soul intervention. It was time for
Bob to come home. The illness was used to bring
Bob to an awareness he could not otherwise
attain.

Bob: That's why I passed from my life. The illness
allowed me finally to overcome the weakness
and fear.

Tricia: How does the Council feel I've done in terms of
learning about and forgiving abandonment and
betrayal? Is there more for me to do?

"Milton is reassuring me," Tricia told me. "I'm feeling a wave
of love from all of them."

Milton: There's such love for you. There's no judgment.
Everything you have done and will do is divinely
orchestrated, accepted, and never wrong.

Tricia: How can I release any guilt I still feel about the
way I reacted, any anger I still feel toward myself
[for reacting that way], and any jealousy I still
feel toward Claire?

Entera: The personality is necessary as a catalyst for
[soul] growth. Realizing this will help you to
release guilt and jealousy, which are both fear-
based.

"Now she's showing me the rest of the Council to impress
upon me the gift of being here."

Entera: You are more than the personality in a life, but
the personality is to be respected, admired,
and encouraged because that's why you come
into a life: to be a human and have emotions,
to feel feelings. This allows you to grow and

is a gift to your soul. That's the purpose of your lives. It should be celebrated, not feared or condemned.

"I feel such love and acceptance from them all. They're telling me that I'm doing a wonderful job and that I can't do any wrong. No choices would be wrong, and I didn't harm Bob; I helped him. That's so meaningful to me."

Tricia: How do you feel about everything that hap-
[to Bob]   pened? How do you feel about me now?

"He just squeezed my hand. It's like he's joking with me, saying without speaking something like, 'If you don't know by now how much I love you . . .'"

Bob: You must look at the plan as mission accomplished.

"He's laughing. They're all smiling. It's beautiful, so beautiful."

Tricia: Will we incarnate together again? Will you wait for me so we can do that?

Bob: Yes on both counts.

Tricia: What else would you like me to understand?
[to the Council]

Milton: The courage you and Bob had to plan and create this life together, a life with such pain and such joy. Pain is personal, productive, and subjective in a lifetime.

Tricia: What is Claire's relationship to me? Is she in my soul group? Have I had other lives with her?

A soul group is a collection of souls who are at approximately the same vibration and evolutionary stage. The members of a soul group take turns playing every conceivable role for one another across many lifetimes.

Milton: Yes, she is in your soul group. She was in a lifetime with Bob as his twin sister. You were not in that lifetime, but you have had lifetimes with her. She was your father in a lifetime.

Tricia: Why didn't I have a full lifetime with Bob? Why did we meet as we did? Why have I felt so much more love for him than anyone else in my life, almost like a worship?

Entera: The meeting was set so that Bob could have much of this life facing his weakness and have other significant moments before you met. The meeting was planned to be when it was. It would not have worked the same if you met earlier.

The love comes from a soul connection of many lives together. You will have lives together that occur simultaneously. The love will always be there. Nothing will ever harm it.

I understood Entera's reference to simultaneous lives to mean that Tricia and Bob will have parallel selves together in parallel dimensions. The reference to simultaneity also served for me as a confirmation that Tricia was truly talking with her Council because simultaneity and non-linearity describe the true nature of the cosmos. Linear time, by contrast, is an illusion of the third dimension, an illusion created by the limitations of the five senses and the human brain.

Tricia: I miss you, Bob.

Bob: I'm with you. I'm always with you. You can hear me. I haven't left you. I will always be with you. I will remind you [that I'm there].

Tricia: Bob, thank you. You gave me a life I couldn't even have imagined. Thank you for all your love, your devotion, and your sweet nature. Thank you so very, very much for everything.

I want you to know that I have never stopped loving you. There has never been a moment I haven't loved you. Even when I was saying things I knew were hurting you, I loved you, and I tried to stop.

Bob: I know.

"He's so filled with love!" Tricia exclaimed again. "There are so many smiles now, so much reassurance. I think there's nothing I can say that he doesn't already know. I'm so anxious to hold him again."

Bob: I remember it all. I remember how we would hold each other and say we were in heaven. I live in your heart.

"I feel so much love and acceptance. Now Bob is getting up."

Bob: I will be leaving, but I've never really left.

"He's squeezing my hand and walking away."

Milton: Your pre-birth plan has been fulfilled.

Entera: But, your life has more to give, and you have more to give. Within your plan there was a hope that you would surpass doubt and get to a place of belief in yourself. That's [the purpose of] the continuation of your existence as Tricia. Now, just believe it.

Tricia: What is the "more" I'm to give?

Entera: To express what you've learned through compassion and listening, to express your knowing without fear.

Tricia: How do I move from doubt to belief in myself?

Milton: When you write, you edit yourself.

"He's showing me a visual of when I write. I change it and change it."

Milton: Stop editing yourself [in life]. Believe what you're saying.

Tricia: Should I take action in some way or just allow life to come?

Entera: Life runs most smoothly in a flow. Allow life to come to you. There's not-doing as living.

Tricia: My body is aging. Is there something I should do to extend my life or make my body healthier?

Entera: The body follows consciousness. The body follows joy or fear. Follow joy, and the body will follow.

Tricia: Where did my eating disorder come from? What is the best way to cope with it?

Milton: It comes from feeling starved for attention, starved for meaning, and fearful of not being accepted.

Entera: Food is a joy, but it cannot fulfill the soul.

"She's showing me music, meditation, and acceptance of myself without fear."

Tricia: Why do I only see three of you when I know that there are nine more?

Milton and Entera: We are your guides for this journey. There is no need for you to visualize the others. They're here, and you can feel them and their love.

I asked Tricia if she now felt complete in talking with the Council.

"Other than expressing my gratitude for their help and over-whelming love and acceptance of me, yes. I wish I had the words, but I know they can feel my deep appreciation for bringing Bob to me. I'm so grateful for the opportunity to see him looking so radiant and feeling his nearness again. Thank you. Thank you." I was moved by the impassioned way in which Tricia spoke.

I guided her focus back into her physical body, bringing her back gradually and gently.

"Oh, wow!" she said suddenly as she opened her eyes. "I didn't even know I had tears—now they're running down my cheeks."

"Tricia, what parts about the experience stood out to you?"

"Bob," she said without hesitation, "I'm amazed. I didn't think I would see him there, and I didn't expect him to look or feel the way he did. It was the best part of him that I've always felt and known, but when you're living life, you feel a lot of other parts, too. It's astounding! And the feel of his hands on mine—my hands were tingling all the way through. It was like an electrical pulse. And the faces of those wonderful beings—almost alien, beautiful, ethereal.

"Also, it was very good for me to realize—and I don't want to forget—that Claire is beloved by the whole soul group, and to not look at her as this invader into a life that was good until she came along, but more as a catalyst, a friend.

"This experience has lifted me. I'm just sitting here in this big puddle of gratitude. And that's from my heart."

Tricia's Session with Corbie

To expand upon what we had learned in her regressions, Tricia and I had a session with medium Corbie Mitleid, who has a particular gift for channeling people's souls (higher selves). Because a soul consists of all the personalities it has ever created, a soul will sometimes refer to itself as "we" or "us" when speaking through Corbie. Both Tricia and I were excited to see what Spirit would share with us.

"Mother/Father God," Corbie began, "thank you for giving me the opportunity to be of service today. Surround us with your unconditional light of love, protection, wisdom, compassion, service, and truth. May only truth be spoken. May only truth be heard. Let me be a clear mirror to bring Tricia, Bob, Claire, and Rob the information that is sought today. May I remain always head, hands, and heart completely in your service. In the name of the Christ this is done. Amen.

"I'm seeing three luminescent souls pull out chairs and sit at a round table," Corbie announced. "They are coming in specifically to talk with us today."

"I want to begin by thanking the three beings who have joined us," I said. "Are we talking with the souls of Tricia, Bob, and Claire?"

"We have agreed to hold hands in faith and compassion that this work will serve you," came the reply, which I took as yes. As always when Corbie channels, her voice had suddenly deepened, and her speech had slowed and became more halting and deliberate. "We are here and glad to be asked."

"I'd like to ask Tricia's higher self," I continued, "did you plan before Tricia was born for her to be in relationship with Bob and for Bob to have an intimate relationship with Claire? If so, why?"

"This is the higher self of Tricia. We agreed, Bob and I, that our bond was strong enough to allow this incursion in this life.

We three know each other well. This was not a stranger barging into our life uninvited. It was service. It was love. We three love each other, and so the blending of lives is always healing when the lives are seen outside of time, as if finishing another chapter in a book you love. This life was a chapter—no more.

"You [humans] believe that there is not enough love to go around," Tricia's higher self added. "An affair is seen as 'I am not loved enough. I am not enough.' It is difficult when in the body surrounded by rules and noise to understand this, but no soul looks at another and says, 'You must not have celestial congress with that other soul.' We know that we are infinite. Why set boundaries? It is something we so wish people would understand."

"Are you saying it's OK for anyone who would like to have an affair to have one?" I wondered. I asked not in disapproval or challenge, but simply to clarify.

"You say 'OK' as if it is permission. Does one want to learn within the construct of the world one has chosen to reincarnate in? Perhaps not. If one is sufficiently connected to All That Is, that rule [monogamy] may be held loosely. Having an affair, as you put it, is only a difficulty when the boundaries of duality are likely to trigger other lessons. In this, Tricia's lessons are forgiveness and the understanding of the Love that reaches out to all three souls. The forgiveness may not just be for Bob or Clair, as the personality Tricia may wish to learn to forgive herself for any jealously, anger, or hurt.

"All of it is a shade and hue of the duality that pulls the soul away from unconditional love. Unconditional love is just that: there is no condition that would take away the feelings of love and acceptance among the three souls. That is what we all hope for someday when we are in the body. This is but a step on the road."

"You mentioned that Tricia is learning lessons about forgiveness and love," I said. "How do you feel she has done in this lifetime in regard to learning those lessons?"

"When you ask that of us, the vision is this: The boat may be in stormy water and spray may be in her face, but she is strong.

She will make the voyage to peace. We gave her depth, vision, and tenacity. These things will help her to heal from any perceived betrayal."

With that, Tricia jumped into the conversation.

"Why am I still in this life?" she asked her higher self. Her tone conveyed genuine interest, not resistance. "And what do I have to give in the rest of my life?"

"Dearest, every lesson you succeed in learning before you rejoin us can be spread like wildflower seeds to others. You may meet someone whose situation is as yours, but they are still enraged. They still rail at God. They still hate the ones they perceive as having betrayed them. We have been working on this in many lives, and while you may not remember them, the learning has been gifted to you. Also, until you are both feet in the grave, love may once more beckon and you may choose to live that love. There are more lessons than the main one."

"When I was reacting in anger toward Bob," Tricia replied, "he was so remorseful that he over-compensated by adoring me in a way he never had. I suggested that was guilt. He swore that he just saw me for the first time and that this was a love that had nothing to do with guilt. I've always wondered if this was true." As Tricia spoke, I heard in her voice her deep longing for Bob.

"The adoration was truth," her soul affirmed. "There was no falsehood in how much he loved you. You would have had the same deepening had you accepted Claire and the three of you had become joined, though in your time and space that can be difficult. Because humanity is taught scarcity, you do not believe that three can share; it must be two. If it is three, one will lose."

"Rob," Corbie said, her voice suddenly back to its usual tone. "Now Bob's soul is coming in with a vision. I see feet walking on wet sand. When Bob first returned Home, he found comfort walking on lonely beaches that he created, listening quietly to the surf and allowing it to lull him. His soul will now speak."

"Just as the footprints are washed away, may any hurt be washed away from Tricia," Bob's soul offered. (Corbie's speech had slowed once again.) "We hope that as we are drawn further down the path, there will be an opportunity that as three loving adults we may find unconditional love. Love is not necessarily sex. Love can be, 'I am you.' Love can be, 'It is my hope and desire to see your life joyful. Let me be part of it.'"

I then asked Bob's soul to speak to those who have had an affair and who feel remorse, regret, or self-judgment.

"Forgiveness is potent medicine not only for the one being forgiven but also for the one who forgives," his soul told us. "Forgiveness is like the wave that washes away the footprints in the sand. To all of you reading: The most important thing is not to beat your breast, rend your clothing, or cut yourself to bleed with pain. It is to be forgiven and to love honestly. Turn your regret and remorse into a self-promise that love throughout the rest of your particular existence will be unconditional no matter what the circumstances. That will include yourself. Loving yourself after what is perceived as a transgression does not mean that the transgression is not bothersome to the personality. It means that your humanity, your 'flawed' behaviors that are required to learn in the Earth school, are accepted, the lessons learned. The 'flaws' are felt, but then like the schoolbook you have finished, it can be closed shut.

"Tricia," I said, "what else would you like to ask?"

"I would like to ask Claire's higher self if Claire understands that I'm grateful for the learning that's come from this experience and that there is forgiveness in my heart. I have felt the sisterhood between us, but I wasn't able to speak that to her because I don't see her. I want to make sure at least her higher self is aware of that and can get that through to her."

"Never fear," Claire's soul assured. "All of the love, all of the tenderness, all of the compassion that you wish to give to Claire's personality comes through us, and though she may not be able to accept it from you directly, this indirect route is as good. It will help to heal that personality of its own anguish, for part of that personality has not yet come to terms with the one who passed. It is to be hoped that Claire's personality will understand this so that she may have a fulfilling relationship of her own before she transitions. Your love and forgiveness make that more possible because they open and heal her."

I then asked Tricia's soul for some healing words for those whose partner has had or is having an affair and who feel hurt, betrayed, or angry.

"The most difficult thing," advised Tricia's soul, "is when a person sees the partner's affair as a failure. Even should the partner act that way, it does not mean [one has failed]. It means that the partner may not see completely. No person whose partner has an affair must take it as a mark of their lesser being. There are lessons. It could be that the lesson is needed by the partner. Remember, you see things from a two-dimensional viewpoint. We, here, understand that if a personality is the pained party, it can often be that it volunteered to be the shattered mirror the partner must gaze at, accepting that it was the partner's hand that shattered the mirror. Whether or not that partner learns the lesson is not up to the one who agrees to be the mirror. It is only when you believe that another's action was done because you forced that partner to do it that the lesson—all truth—is lost."

"Is there anything else Tricia's, Bob's, or Claire's soul would like to share with readers?"

"This is Tricia's higher self, speaking for all of us. Love is not confined to shapes. Love is not confined to construct. Long, long ago you learned that all are one. 'How can that be?' you say. 'I don't love the other. How can the left hand burn the right?' That is the connection—the soul connection—we all have with one another. We three have explored love, forgiveness, and boundaries of many lives and will continue to do so. We are like the beautiful flower that shapes and reshapes itself from year to year. We are the bulb that sleeps in the ground in winter and then blooms again. The bulb has one flower, perhaps another the next year. It does not say to the flower next to it, 'Because I am a yellow tulip and you are a pink crocus, something is not right.' We are flowers. We all grow from the same soil. We all need nourishment, sun, and rain—or for the soul, the shining light of love and the tears of forgiveness.

"We all three extend such gratitude to those three brave incarnations who sought to learn the lessons. We are greater for their willingness to step into a world of duality and the finite that we may have infinite singularity here. Blessings on all three for their generosity to us."

∽

Tricia returned to Spirit from the past life she saw without having forgiven Bob for leaving her. What we leave unhealed in the past we plan to heal in the future. Tricia chose to carry energetically into body the energy of unforgiveness, not for the purpose of expressing it but rather for the purpose of transmuting it.

How may Tricia do that? "Stop resisting who you truly are," her spirit guide Reeding advises. Like each of us, Tricia is a being made by love, from love, and for love. When we come into body and step behind the veil of forgetfulness, we forget this eternal truth. Conditioning, the vast majority of which is at the subconscious or unconscious level, takes over. We are conditioned to believe that life is hard and requires hard work. Some of us are taught that happiness is not right and not who we really are.

Too, when we are behind the veil and in a state of perceived separation, ego rises to the forefront. Ego tells us that we must defend ourselves from those who have betrayed us. Yet defense requires a focus on attack and therefore calls attack to us. As *A Course in Miracles* tells us, "In my defenselessness my safety lies." For only in complete defenselessness is attack not foreseen and therefore not attracted.

How do we overcome conditioning and ego? "Remember how to play," Reeding tells Tricia. "Remember who you were as a child. Bob came to teach you that. He was a teacher of playfulness. Remember how much fun it can be to play." How perfect, then, that Bob, the "cause" of unforgiveness in the past life and rage earlier in the present life, is himself a source of their healing. Bob's love for Tricia was so great that he agreed to provide not only the opportunity for her to learn forgiveness but also one pathway to that destination. When we plan our greatest challenges before we are born, we gift to ourselves—and others gift to us—that which we will need to surmount them.

The plan to experience infidelity in their marriage was intended to benefit Bob as much as Tricia. Both saw this experience as providing the opportunity and the motivation to move from fear to love. Tricia moved from a fear of abandonment to forgiveness and gratitude; likewise, Bob moved from a fear of not pleasing others to a greater sense of sovereignty. Fears are often best resolved by "kissing them on the nose," and Bob planned to do just that when he agreed in their pre-birth planning to the extramarital affair. He knew this affair would likely enrage Tricia. For a "pleaser" to agree to such a plan is an act of courage. Bob was able to summon such great courage only because behind it is his great, everlasting love for Tricia.

Just as Bob agreed to the infidelity as an act of love and service to Tricia, so, too, did Claire. Claire is a member of their soul group, a collective of souls who are at more or less the same vibration or stage of evolution. Out of love the members of a soul group take turns playing every conceivable role with and for one another: parent and child, brother and sister, best of friends, and even mortal enemies. At the soul level there is no judgment of any role; rather, the soul views all roles as opportunities for expansion, healing, service, and the cultivation of wisdom and virtues. On the Earth plane little is as it seems: Our greatest tormentors in the physical are often those in our soul group with whom we share the strongest love, the longest history, and the greatest trust. Tricia knew before she was born that the role of betrayal is best played by those she trusts most.

Her healing complete, Tricia may now be of service to Claire. As Claire's soul told us, all of the love, tenderness, and compassion Tricia wishes to give to Claire may be transmitted to her through her soul. In the physical realm, due to the limitations of the five senses we appear to be separate beings in distinct bodies. In reality all minds are joined and each of us is a cell in the body of one Divine Being. The forgiveness Tricia has cultivated is felt and known by Claire at levels below conscious awareness. The love Tricia sends to her helps her to heal from Bob's death and even makes another loving, romantic relationship more likely.

What, then, to do with the knowledge that infidelity is planned before birth? An awareness of pre-birth planning is not to be used as a spiritual bypass. Wounds are healed as emotions are allowed and felt, ideally without resistance or judgment. For you who feel you have been betrayed, know this: Any anger or rage you feel is valid. Feel it deeply and freely for as long as it calls to be felt. Let an understanding of life plans abide quietly in your mind and heart; it will be there for you when you are ready.

On the Earth plane, we humans are engaged in the process of purification or clarification: We are blends of light and dark, love and fear, ever seeking to release darkness and fear and move further toward light and love. This alchemy takes myriad forms, only one of which is infidelity. Yet the content of each form is the same: the learning of how better to give and receive love. Such is the touchstone of our life plans.

CHAPTER 2

Impotence

IMPOTENCE AND OTHER FORMS OF sexual dysfunction are common among both men and women. Studies show that by age 40, 5 percent of all men experience complete erectile dysfunction. By age 70 that increases to 15 percent. Mild and moderate erectile dysfunction affects approximately 10 percent of men per decade of life (i.e., 50 percent of men in their 50s, 60 percent of men in the 60s). Among pre-menopausal women, 41 percent experience some form of sexual dysfunction.

The effects are difficult at best and devastating at worst. Those who experience impotence often feel defective. Frequently, they experience shame and guilt for "letting their partner down." The strain can break a relationship. Quite naturally people wonder why this is happening, what it means, and how to heal and move forward.

To understand whether impotence is planned before birth, I spoke with Andrew, who was courageous enough to share his experiences with me.

Andrew

At the time of our conversation, Andrew was thirty-six and living in Belfast, Northern Ireland. He was working for a charity

for the homeless and ran its drop-in shelter for refugees and asylum seekers.

"Around the age of twenty-six," he began, "I started to rapidly
lose my hair. It really affected my confidence, self-esteem, and
ability to enter relationships with girls. So I contacted a hair loss
transplant specialist. He explained that I would take a prescription
medication for a number of months. It would slow the hair loss,
and then there would be the possibility of having a hair transplant.

"I remember specifically saying that I'd heard this medication
can affect libido. He said, 'That's in a very small percentage, and
because you're so young, it's very unlikely to happen. Even if it
does, if you just stop taking it, your libido will be back to normal
within a month.' I still felt trepidation about it, but I started taking the tablets. It was about five days before I realized that it had
affected my libido and getting an erection."

"Andrew, what specifically did you experience?"

"No sexual drive and total inability to get any erection whatsoever," he replied. "It was like a death sentence, like seeing my
whole dream and future disintegrating before me—no wife, no
children. I remember just sitting there, the tears coming down
and contemplating suicide. I found a lot of online forums where
there were people who had done the same thing as myself, and
five and ten years later were saying that they were still totally
impotent. That was crushing."

From that point things became even more difficult for
Andrew. His employer suffered a financial setback and decided
he could no longer afford to keep Andrew on staff. In his personal life, his sexual challenges caused him to end a promising
new relationship with a woman, someone about whom he had
been very excited.

"It seemed my life was over," he said sadly. "I plunged into a
deep, dark depression."

Andrew moved in with his parents. For a year or so he seldom
left their home. He lost contact with friends and was plagued by
thoughts of suicide. Psychiatrists, antidepressants, and sleeping
pills were no help. Then a new perspective began to emerge.

"I came to the point where I realized I wasn't going to kill myself, so I may as well try to do something with it." He started reading voraciously about spirituality. He took courses in healing. He volunteered at the refugee center and six months later was hired to run it. His work there brought about even bigger changes in his viewpoint.

"The center is for destitute migrants," he explained. "There I saw people who had totally given up on themselves and on life, which is what I had done. They're over here on their own. With their language problems they can't find work, so they eventually turn to alcohol and are on the street. I saw how lucky I was. I had a roof over my head. I had a loving family. As I was helping the migrants, I was helping myself. The more I was able to do that, the more my life transformed."

A couple of years passed. Andrew then met Sarah, a Canadian studying in Belfast. He felt she was the woman of his dreams.

"She was everything I'd ever wanted in a woman and more," he recalled. "She was inspirational, creative, attractive. We connected on every level. But there was this feeling of 'What can I do with this?' I didn't feel confident enough to tell her. I couldn't get into a relationship because of this. She's now married to someone else," he said softly.

Since that time Andrew has discovered that he can have sexual intercourse if he takes Viagra, and he is now more optimistic about finding a life partner. He also feels that tremendous growth has resulted from his suffering. "Because of the pain I've gone through I am able to sit with refugees, asylum seekers, and the homeless, be present with them, validate their pain, who they are, and their experience," he told me.

When Andrew first agreed to speak with me for this book, he said he believed he had planned before birth to have the experience with the medication and the resulting low libido and impotence. "Andrew," I asked, "do you think you planned this in part so that you could be of service to the refugees?"

"I'm now of the view that it has to be that way," he answered, certainty in his voice. "It feels right and it feels true." Andrew's use of the word *feel* was meaningful to me. I took it to indicate that he is listening to his intuition, which is one of the ways in which Spirit communicates with us. Feelings are the language of the soul.

Too, I suspected that Andrew's insight about one of the purposes of his experience was right on the mark. When we plan before birth to have a significant challenge in the upcoming lifetime, we do so in part to cultivate and then express certain qualities that are important to our souls. Andrew had clearly deepened in compassion, empathy, and gratitude, but simply cultivating such qualities would not be sufficient from his soul's perspective. His soul would also want to have the experience of expressing the virtues he had developed. For the soul such expression creates feelings of expansion and joy.

"This experience has been life transforming," Andrew continued. "I've learned so much about life, myself, the soul, humans, connection, and how something good can come from suffering. When I was in a dark time I remember praying, and the words of a song came to me: *'I want to know what love is, and I want you to show me.'* This whole process was showing me what love is. On the drive to work, I send love to the next car or to people as I go by them. At work I just keep sending love. It's about giving and giving and giving from that endless place, which is our true nature. Who we are is love. I've had an actual experience and physical realization of this, not someone telling me."

"After this lifetime is over, when you're back on the other side and you meet with the man who gave the medication to you, what will you say to him?"

Andrew burst into laughter. "I'll say, *'Thank you! Thank you!'* Rob, there's no animosity, not even any hint of animosity. There's just gratitude: gratitude for changing my life, putting me on a different path, and playing his part."

"Andrew, your story will be read by people who may be in agony due to impotence or low libido. Perhaps they feel victimized by life or by the universe. They may not see deeper spiritual meaning or purpose in it. What would you say to them?"

"I was stuck in that for so long," he acknowledged. "If you think of all the planets in the cosmos and how they rotate in perfect synchronicity; how the ocean, the waves, the moon, the sun, and the stars are all in perfect flow; how the seasons come and go in perfect time; how the sun always rises and falls; and the very fact that we breathe out the life force for the trees and what the trees expel as waste is our life force—it's all in perfect flow yet we somehow think our life isn't in this same perfect flow.

"If you read up about people who are really inspirational," he continued, "the majority have gone through unbearable suffering. So, just be open to the possibility that perhaps you have agreed to go through this for some higher reason. Effectively, all the higher reason comes down to is a greater understanding and expanse of your true nature, which is love. As Wayne Dyer used to say, 'As you change the way you look at things, the things you look at change.'"

I asked how his libido is now.

"It has improved," he said, "but there is still the deep pain and suffering from it. But, I now use this suffering as fuel for the furnace, to push and inspire me to live from love."

Andrew's Between Lives Soul Regression

I was moved and inspired by my conversation with Andrew. His suffering had been immense, yet he had used that suffering to cultivate deep compassion and empathy. He had then taken those virtues and turned them outward in service to others. It seemed very likely he had planned the impotence and low libido before birth in part to have the motivation and capacity to help the destitute migrants. I wondered, though, what other intentions had played a role in Andrew's planning and what else he had sought to learn or do. I hoped his regression would shed light on these questions.

I took Andrew through the usual physical and mental relaxation steps, then guided him through a tunnel from which he emerged into a past life.

"I'm on the steps of my home, just about to go out," he began. "It's day[time]. It's hot."

"I'd like to get a sense of how you're dressed," I said. "What, if anything, do you have on your feet?"

"Sandals."

"As you move up your body, what is covering your legs?"

"Nothing on my lower legs, but there's a red robe or cape, almost like grass material. Then above that there's a shield of golden armor. I have a sword and shoulder pads as well."

"Very good," I replied. "Now, I want you to see yourself standing in front of a mirror so you can see what you look like. I want you to look closely at your face and hair and tell me if you are male or female."

"Male," Andrew answered, "about thirty-five [years old]. My hair is black, my face swarthy. It's a longish face and strong jaw."

"Do you have any expression on your face?"

"I'm angry. Very angry."

"Now, look at your skin. What is your skin color?"

"A mixture between white and brown."

"Are you a small, medium, or large person?"

"Large. I'm powerful and muscular."

I instructed Andrew to allow the mirror to dissolve and the scene to unfold naturally.

"I have a sword," he described. "There are people around me going into hysterics, telling me not to do it. I'm going to get vengeance with someone.

"I go over to my brother's house. I'm screaming. We're shouting at each other, and I kill him."

"Look closely on your brother's face," I prompted. "Do you recognize this soul as anyone who is with you in your current lifetime?"

"My older brother, John. He's done something to betray me, something about telling lies to do with my wife or partner. I killed him for that betrayal. I knew once I did it that I'd be taken to my death. Soldiers are rushing in, and they're taking me away."

"Andrew, I want you to trust that your soul and guides are showing you this scene for a particular reason or reasons. What is important for you to know or understand about the scene you're being shown? Trust that you know the answer."

"It's to do with impotency," he explained. "Having my power taken away from me by a force outside me, a force I loved and who betrayed me. Before I committed that act, I thought he was taking away my power through betrayal, but through seeking vengeance I gave away my power and made myself impotent."

I prompted Andrew to move forward to the next significant event or scene in the same lifetime.

"I'm going to my death," he said as the image came into focus in his mind. "I'm walking through crowds. People are shouting at me. I go into a big courtyard. I'm being led there."

"How do you feel as this is happening?"

"Strange—I actually feel calm. I know this isn't the real end. I also know . . . it's almost a dance between us that had to be completed. It feels fulfilled, even though it's unbelievably horrible."

"Allow the scene to continue. What happens next?"

"I go up to be hung. They put a noose around my neck. There's screaming and shouting and taunting. My hands are tied. I'm standing there, and I know that the stool is about to be kicked. Then there is peace. It is done."

I then took several minutes to guide Andrew's consciousness out of the body in the past life and back Home to the other side.

"What are you experiencing now?" I asked when I thought he was here.

"Being lifted upward . . . an expansion . . . drawing toward light . . . peace . . ." Andrew was now speaking much more slowly and there was a palpable calm in his voice.

"Continue upward," I instructed, "higher and higher . . . farther and farther away from Earth . . . more and more into the light. Tell me what is happening now."

"I'm surrounded and encompassed with unbelievably bright light . . . *there's so much light!*" he exclaimed, now suddenly excited. "It feels natural."

"Andrew, do you sense either that the light itself is a living consciousness or that there are beings within the light?"

"There are now beings in front of me. One in the middle steps up and walks around the edge of a table and comes toward me. It's a being of total light so there is no real form. It's hard to describe. It's almost like this being has a cloak of light around it."

"What does this being's energy feel like?"

"Eternal, knowing, loving, nonjudgmental, familiar."

"I want you to thank this being for stepping forward to talk with you. Then ask this being his or her name and relationship to you. Tell me what answer you receive."

Elar: I'm your spirit guide. My name is Elar [ee-lar]. I'm glad you've come. We've been waiting for you. This is part of what you've been waiting for as well.

I then prompted Andrew to ask Elar several questions. Andrew repeated everything Elar replied:

Andrew: Why was I shown that particular past life?

Elar: It was to be a balancing and harmonizing of previous acts between you and your brother. But, you both carried residual judgment over into Spirit and then took that into this [current] life to be resolved. The residual was judgment of yourselves. Even though your acts were agreed beforehand, there was not self-forgiveness or self-acceptance. Today your impotence is tied to that life, that act. You believed you abused your power, so [by pre-birth design] there's no way to abuse power in this [current] life.

Andrew: How can I now reclaim my power?

Elar:	Know that this is what had to happen. Allow it to be released. Allow yourself to forgive yourself.
Andrew:	How do I do that?
Elar:	Write yourself letters about self-forgiveness, self-compassion, self-worth, and self-love. You are blocking yourself from accepting what you already are. Writing these letters will remind you on a subconscious level of the agreements in that life and bring you to a place where you can fully let them go and appreciate the grand scheme: that *both* parties were willing to dance the dance and play the role.
Andrew:	What else should I write in these letters?
Elar:	Write a letter to your brother's Higher Self asking forgiveness. Then allow your brother's Higher Self to write a letter back to you. Also, write a letter of forgiveness of your brother's acts. Then allow your Higher Self to write a response to that letter.

I noted Elar's repeated use of the word *allow*. The thoughts of the egoic mind are like a static between dimensions. When the mind quiets in meditation (or potentially meditative activities like long country drives or walks alone in nature), this *allows* nonphysical consciousness to communicate with us.

Andrew:	What else is important for me to know or understand about the past life?
Elar:	Power. Not power over people, but power to draw the power *out of* people. You didn't do it. There could have been a different end, but there was the fear of singing the song, which is very similar to the fear you have in this [current] life.

Let go of that. It's time now to bring forth what you have within to help others.

Andrew: How do I do that?

Elar: The power is in the pain. Connect to that. Write from that. Start small, just sharing with people. Be vulnerable and share the fear. That is where the true connection is. It is in the vulnerability, in the fear, that your power lies. Meet them in the vulnerability. Meet them in your fear because they, too, have that fear.

Sensing that Andrew's conversation with Elar had run its course, I felt it was now time for Andrew to visit his Council.

"Andrew," I prompted, "thank Elar for all the love and wisdom he's just shared with you and also for guiding you through your current lifetime. Then tell him that you have other questions you would like to ask your Council of Elders. Now describe what happens next."

"It's almost as if the table has moved," he responded. "It's like a semicircle around me, but not too close."

"How many Council members are there? What do they look like?"

"There are twelve. They are beings of light."

"Do they look or feel male, female, or androgynous?"

"Androgynous."

"What else does their energy feel like?"

"It's all-encompassing, all-knowing energy," Andrew answered, a note of awe in his voice. "Unconditional love and acceptance. They have overseen everything I've been part of. There is nothing they do not know about me, and there is no judgment. There is a lot of love, appreciation, and wonder both ways."

This mutuality of love and appreciation was something I have been told many times. Just as we naturally love and appreciate the very wise and highly evolved beings who oversee our evolution, so, too, do they love and appreciate us for the aspect of

Divinity we truly are.

I asked Andrew to describe the setting.

"It's just pure white light, room-like, but it's hard to even call it that because all is white light. There are some beings over to the right, observing us. I don't have any description for them, just a knowing they are there." Like Andrew, many people report knowing that other beings are present to observe the meeting with the Council.

I prompted Andrew to thank the Council members for being there to talk with him and to ask if one among them would serve as the Council spokesperson.

"Yes," he replied, "the one on the left." Here Andrew began to laugh. "This being is bigger in stature than Elar, more jovial, light-hearted, and uplifting. There's a sense of fun and playfulness between us and all the others."

"Andrew, ask the Council spokesperson his or her name."

"They've already told me. That's why I was laughing, because the name is Iknow. They're all laughing, because they're saying, 'I know Iknow.' That's the being's name."

"How is that spelled?"

"Literally, I-k-n-o-w, like how we would spell it as one word. It's almost like a playful thing."

Although some people find the Council to be serious, many experience them as lighthearted and playful, just as Andrew now is. Indeed, one of the most common messages people receive from Council is to take themselves and life less seriously and to have more fun.

I then prompted Andrew to ask Iknow a long series of questions, beginning with: "What message does the Council have for me today?"

Iknow: We're excited you've come. This is something you've been waiting for on numerous levels.

We commend you for how you've handled your challenges, and we remind you of your willingness to embark on such challenges. We and numerous others have been impressed.

The reminder that Andrew had willingly set himself on a challenging path was important. Because the veil between dimensions causes almost everyone to forget the pre-birth plan, many fall into victim consciousness, the lowest frequency a human can experience. Remembering that we ourselves chose the difficult experiences pulls us out of that vibration and empowers us to learn in a much more conscious and less painful manner.

Andrew: Is there anything additional the Council wants me to know about the past life?

Iknow: There was a possibility of transcendence in that life—to transcend everything that happened, to transcend to love. That would have transcended your brother's acts. It's like wiping the slate clean.

That is possible in every life. The way to do that is always to choose love. No matter what, always choose love. No matter what, just choose love.

Often, the doorway to love and transcendence is through fear—fear of vulnerability, isolation, and rejection. On the other side of that door of fear is love—great, unconditional, never-ending, unjudging, not-moving love. Meet people at that door so they can meet you in their fear. Speak of this fear. Speak of this vulnerability, this lack of love, this not knowing, this not being good enough, this 'who am I to stand before you and say this?'

There they will meet you. There love will be found.

Whether you do it in front of one or a thousand, it's the same.

Andrew: What is my true self?

Iknow: Your true self is love. Don't worry about forgetting [it]; that means there's another beautiful remembering.

Andrew: Why have I not yet met my soulmate?

Iknow: You know a song with the words, 'Come to me. Come to me, wild and free.' [You will meet her] when you are ready to come to her, wild and free. Feel wild and embrace your fear. Embrace your insecurities, your lack of self-love—not to change or get rid of them, but in the knowing that is what makes you human, for nearly every human who ever walked the face of the Earth had these in some form or another.

Be wild and open and free. Live from that free self. It will happen. You don't need to know when or how. It will happen.

Andrew: I'd like to ask about Sarah. I never connected with another woman the way I did with her. What can you tell me about Sarah?

Iknow: You were never supposed to be together [long-term]. You know deep down that is the case; otherwise, you would have put that extra effort in rather than holding back and letting the Universe decide. Know that what needed to be done was done to perfection. Amen.

Andrew: What is a soulmate?

Iknow: A soulmate could be described as the other side of the same coin: the ability to look the opposite

way but always be united as one. In a way it's
the uniting back to Source [God] that you never
[really] left. It is the harmonizing, the perfect
alignment. It is the beauty of you in another and
another in you. It is union.

Andrew: How will I recognize my soulmate when I find
her?

Iknow: You will know without any doubt, like you feel
in your body now. You feel in your body the resonance of our words, our message, our embrace,
our love. There will be no denying. It will be the
presence, the meeting, the eyes, the connection,
the union.

Ask Iknow, does he know? Of course he does.

Andrew: Why did I take the medication? Was it part of
my pre-birth plan to have it affect my penis and
libido? How do I fix that?

Iknow: Yes, it was decided before birth. Part of the
reason is what you've discovered of the previ-
ous life. After you took your brother's life, just
before your death, the disempowerment, the
impotence—in a way what was done was done
to yourself.

But, it has more to do with the higher calling
for this [current] life: awakening to your true
essence, reclaiming your power, because ultimately all power is yours. You are the power, and
this is the life to reclaim the power.

You are now at the precipice of what you came
into this life for. Everything has led to this
point, and everything—all the past, all the
darkness, the medication, and everything else in

between—was with the intention to get to this point. You are now standing where you hoped you would stand before you took your very first breath.

It is so beautiful, if only you could know. If only you could know. We commend you.

Andrew: If my intentions were to heal the giving away of my power in the past life and to reclaim my power in my current lifetime, why plan experiences of impotence and low libido? Why not just plan to be a very powerful person?

Iknow: There was fear that if you were a very powerful person, you would abuse this power, which was your misconceived belief in the past life and the reality of lives before that.

Also, if you come in or spend your whole life as a person of power, there's disconnect, misunderstanding, and lack of empathy for the humanness of fear, the no-way-to-go-on, the abyss of hopelessness. If you haven't walked that path, how can you meet another person there? You can't stand at that door, hold that door open, and be the doorman for others to walk through.

You agreed for this [current] life to have a true understanding of what it's like to be the opposite of your true self. Then in the returning you can take others with you. You can step down into hell and walk with them hand in hand.

Here Iknow had beautifully described the life plan of a lightworker. A lightworker seeks to experience firsthand the very thing he wanted before birth to change. Truly powerful change—transformational change—can be affected only *from within the vibration* one seeks to alter. Here was the great paradox of Andrew's pre-birth plan: only by first making himself impotent could he become truly powerful. Andrew's was a classic learning-through-opposites plan in which the contrast between impotence and true, soul-based power would help him to appreciate and truly understand his immense power as a Divine Being.

Andrew: In what other ways have the experiences of impotence and low libido served me in my current life?

Iknow: It was to take away distractions; otherwise, there may have been women, perhaps you having children—distractions of the material plane and getting off the path, which has happened in previous lives.

Also, the harshness, the pain, the suffering won't let you give up. There's no getting off the path now. Feel for the furnace that burns, that pushes, that drives the dream forward: that search for truth and the search to bring others along with you. It was agreed this was the best way, not necessarily easy, but the best way.

It's like pushing a ball under water. The farther you push it, the farther it's going to spring up. Everything has led and continues to lead to a greater understanding through contrast of the true essence, the love.

Andrew: What is the significance of my current work with destitute migrants?

Iknow: Whatever you want for yourself, bring to others first. So, in meeting the homeless, the helpless, the people who have given up, the people who have no love or self-love, then this [love] started to blossom for you. And it has continued to grow and grow and grow. It's all about being there with people, just being with them in presence, not necessarily having or saying that you have any answers. It is recognition of that humanity and also that Divinity.

Here we had come to a crucial point: by first coming into an awareness of his own Divinity, Andrew was then able to see the Divine in others. When others then saw their Divinity reflected in Andrew's eyes, they began to remember who they really are. In this way does true healing occur.

Andrew: The pain in my penis has been a source of massive suffering for me. Is there anything else you can tell me about the reason for the pain or how to heal it?

Iknow: The reasons have been covered. Is there anything else that needs to be said? Just that we are with you. You can call out to us. You can call for our help.

We congratulate and embrace you for being brave enough to walk this path in the name of Love. Have this as your motto from this day forth, a new mantra that is chiseled on you: 'I do this in the name of Love.' That is why you came into this life, in this body, as Andrew Doherty. You knew well that it would be perilous in parts, but there was the yearning to get to that end goal, because effectively you *are* that end goal.

Connect with this in the heart. Amen.

Andrew: How do I do all of this with more grace and ease?

I was jolted when Iknow then exploded in a burst of passion. Andrew relayed not just Iknow's words, but also the tremendous intensity and power with which he imbued them:

Iknow: Surrender all concept of future. Oh, to live without future! Ohhh, I could cry now! Oh, if only you could live this day without the future, you would be in Heaven! For what do you need if you have no future?

There is no future! This is the last moment of your existence! Share now, because if you don't, after your next breath, it's over! There's no future; live from there. Don't do anything for the sake of the future. Do it for the moment. The rose knows no future. The rose knows this moment and this blossom. See the beauty the rose does create.

Share and live like the man who has no future. Embody that, for there is your freedom.

Clearly, Iknow felt he had a key to happiness for the incarnate human, if we would but allow ourselves to utilize it.

Having prompted Andrew to ask all the questions he and I had wanted to explore, and sensing that Iknow's flourish marked the end of his comments, I told Andrew to ask Iknow and the rest of the Council for an energetic healing that would work on all levels—physical, emotional, mental, and spiritual. I instructed Andrew to set an intention to receive the healing fully on all those levels.

When Andrew indicated the healing was complete, I brought him slowly out of the trance state.

"WOW!" he exclaimed.

"What was that like for you?" I asked.

"How long have you got?" he said with a laugh. "*It was absolutely amazing on so many levels!* The knowledge that was coming through and how it was all making sense . . . it's exactly what I've been searching for, to be honest. It's like the final piece of the jigsaw puzzle. I can't thank you enough—really can't.

"It's good to see there's a reason for everything I went through," Andrew continued with a tone of relief, "and knowing it's the fear that is the meeting point. That's perfect. And 'I do this in the name of Love' and 'Surrender all concept of future,' which is powerful. This is sacred work, and it's life-changing for me!

"It's all about a different perspective, knowing that this [impotence and low libido] isn't wrong, that I agreed to do this. Ultimately, it's about choosing Love. It's about choosing Love."

Andrew's Between Lives Soul Regression had shed much light on the underlying spiritual meaning and purpose of the impotence and low libido. I now knew the connection between those experiences and one of Andrew's past lives. I also had a sense of what Andrew's other pre-birth intentions had been. But, were there other objectives for the current lifetime that had not been shared by Elar or Iknow? What more could I offer to readers who face the same challenges as Andrew's?

To answer these questions, Andrew and I worked with medium Staci Wells. Prior to the session, I provided Staci with Andrew's full name and birthdate, which her guide would use to access information in the Akashic Record, the complete, nonphysical record of everything relevant to the Earth plane. I also told Staci that Andrew and I would like to receive information about his pre-birth plan with his ex-girlfriend, Sarah.

Andrew's Session with Staci

As the session started, Staci told us that her spirit guide, who does not use a particular name, was speaking to her and that she would relay his words to us.

"Your loneliness is self-enforced," Staci's guide began, speaking to Andrew. "It is created by self and continued by self."

Having talked extensively with Staci's guide in many sessions for my previous two books, I knew this insight was said with love and complete nonjudgment. From the perspective of Staci's guide, it was simply a statement of fact. The implication was clear and to the heart of the matter: notwithstanding the impotence and low libido, it was still possible for Andrew not to be lonely. Staci's guide was reminding Andrew of his innate power as the creator of his experience. The same power lies within each of us.

"You are working on self-love in this lifetime," continued Staci's guide. "You are also working on the attitude of blame [not blaming self or others], and you are learning to temper anger with patience."

Staci's guide then stepped aside so Staci could speak directly with Andrew.

"Your most important karmic lesson is called strengthening adaptiveness. At its heart this lesson is really about emotional flexibility and the ability to bounce back from the storms that happen in life. Andrew, as a soul, life after life, you have noticed that you have a pattern of not dealing very well with disappointment.

"Also, your over-arching effort as a soul is to be a leader and to use your creative instincts and abilities to lead, both in your own life and in the lives of others. A situation presents itself to you so that you will dedicate your life to understanding and integrating it within yourself. By doing so you develop a talent for dealing with it. You are then able to share that with others to get them through their crises, their points of lack of self-forgiveness, self-awareness, and self-understanding."

Here we had come to the service-to-others component of Andrew's life plan. In literally every pre-birth plan I have examined, service to others has always been present in some form. From the perspective of the soul, it is not sufficient simply to cultivate certain virtues or master certain lessons. Our souls always want us to mine the gold in our experiences and then share that wealth with others.

"Andrew," Staci continued, "Spirit is making me aware that you and your spirit guide talked [in your pre-birth planning] about the importance of focusing on the beauty and potential in a given life span—life to life to life. In other words, you have to be careful what you choose to focus on. Do you choose to focus on the pain and suffering, or do you choose to focus on the beauty in your life, beauty that alleviates your suffering and brings satisfaction and contentment to you?"

As Staci posed this important question to Andrew, I reminded myself that Spirit was articulating a fundamental law of the universe: Whatever we pay attention to increases. Resistance to life challenges like impotence and low libido is a form of attention; hence the adage "What we resist persists." How, then, does one cope with or surmount challenges if not by paying attention to them? The answer: by focusing as much as possible on the good that has or can come from the experience.

"You've also been working on the karmic lesson of over-impulsivity," Staci added. "This lesson teaches us the importance of taking care of ourselves, our lives—doing all the things that need to be done so that by the end of our lives we wind up content, healthy, well taken care of.

"So many people with this karmic lesson choose the wrong mate early in life—and sometimes repeatedly through life—because they're under the impression, 'I never felt this way about anybody before! This must be the one!' when really that kind of feeling for somebody with the lesson of over-impulsivity is more of a red flag.

"There are many positive aspects of the karmic lesson of over-impulsivity. Some positive qualities are your heart of gold; the way you feel other people's pain and are ready to do something to help; and your ability to love deeply and wholeheartedly, which like most of us you have not learned to do quite yet with yourself.

"The purpose of the lesson is for you to rise to being able to love unconditionally. In this lifetime it's not just about learning to love others unconditionally; it's most importantly about learning to love *yourself* unconditionally.

"Andrew, your next karmic lesson is balance. The heart of that lesson is to learn to connect with the calm place within.

That place is not in sorrow, not in anger. It's not in 'should have, would have, could have.' It just *is*. If you don't learn to strengthen your connection to that peaceful, calm place within yourself, you're going to be prone to outburst responses to life.

"The next karmic lesson is called self-esteem, self-worth, self-confidence, and self-expression, which equals a refined self-expression. You are learning not to center yourself on the expectations of others. You are trying instead to align yourself with your own expectations of yourself."

With that, Staci and her guide concluded their overview of Andrew's major lessons of life.

"Staci, do you feel ready to go into the pre-birth planning session and listen to the conversation?" I asked.

"Yes," she replied. "Let me see if I can get some words." There was a long pause as she focused.

"Andrew," Staci said as a scene from his pre-birth planning session became clear in her mind, "by this point in your planning session you have already done a review of your other lifetimes, not just the most immediate past life but all your other lifetimes, too. Your guide is talking about a history you have of putting others before yourself. You leave your needs for last, and that contributes to outbursts when you can do it no more and also when you feel that no one has noticed your sacrifice and suffering."

Spirit Guide: Self-love becomes important for you to draw upon. Is that not true?

Andrew: Yes, very much so. I love and learn, live and learn, and then forget to love again. It's the way I ended my life so many lifetimes in a row. I wish to counter this aspect of myself in this lifetime-to-be.

"Now I am witnessing the conversation between Andrew and Sarah. Andrew, she is sitting across from you in the pre-birth planning session. There is a discussion of a lifetime in Canada, where you were brother and sister. She's talking about her need to forgive herself because she feels she deserted you in that life. She became pen pals with a gentleman and went off to the other side of the country to marry him and raise a family. You two never saw each other after that. You lapsed into drugs to ease your loneliness and later took your own life."

Sarah: I forgive you. I forgive you.

"She forgives you for taking your own life," Staci clarified.

Sarah: Who I do not forgive is myself.

I had misgivings from the moment I left you in that life. I knew as I turned my back that I was going into the rest of my life—into the new, the good—and for me it was a parting. I also knew that you would sacrifice without me—that you would not make a lot of good friendships and that you would suffer and struggle—but I held my own happiness higher than yours.

I blame myself.

Andrew: I love you. I never held you responsible for my life or my behavior. I loved you before. I will always love you. This will never change. You have provided safe harbor to me time and time again in so many lives, whether you were my cousin, my lover, my neighbor, or my mother. You have held my hand through the worst of times, but now it's time to let me go, let me carry on. I feel ready this time.

"I see that the two of you bend toward each other and look down at your pre-birth planning chart. You're looking for a time to meet. She suggests the time frame, and you agree."

Sarah: I will be moving on to another, but in knowing me, I hope you, my brother, come to know yourself, for that is the aim and the purpose I hold: that you may know yourself, and that even when you suffer, you may know the light of God and His hand in your life, and come to the sense I have that all is sure, all is certain, and all is right.

And even though we may blindly go into the future [when in body], we hold the faith that all will be well, and so it is. I understand you, my brother. I understand you are still learning how to live this and be in the world without expectations. I know this is a struggle for you. I know there is resistance still in you and avoidance to learning this, but with my love for you at least in your life for a time, I hold in my heart that you can hang on to the experience of what it feels like to be in love inside your heart and carry this with you forever, so that you may feel this for yourself, and fall in love and be in love with yourself over and over again, and learn to love yourself through the hardships in life—the hardships that you have learned to challenge yourself physically with and muster through, but that emotionally still turn you into a wreck.

I hold this challenge for you, my brother. I also hold the unseeking, undying, never-ending, always throughout this universe and the next, the greatest love for you any individual could have.

When you see me, you will know me. You will see the light in my eyes, and the energy will go straight to your heart. You will know me in this way.

Andrew: Yes, yes I will. [puts his hand on his heart chakra.] I know this feeling well, and I know you will have purpose in my life. I may struggle from time to time with that purpose. I may not understand the direction or the why or the challenge, but I hold in my heart that I love you, that I trust you, and that you will always lead me to my best. So be it, and so may it be, always.

"You bow your heads to each other in agreement," Staci added, "but it also carries the energy of respect and love. She gets up and goes back into the gallery, where some of your soul group sit, both to bear witness and to be called into involvement in the planning."

"Staci, can you get the conversation with Andrew's future mother?" I asked. "When the incident with the medication happened, he moved back home. She took care of him and stopped working to do so. It was a tremendous strain on both parents, in particular his mother. I wonder what their plan is and what they talked about."

Again we were silent for a few moments as Staci's guide took her to a particular place in Andrew's Akashic Records.

"I'm coming in on the middle of a conversation between Andrew and his mother in his pre-birth planning session," Staci said. "I see them seated across from each other on the floor with Andrew's planning chart between them. His mother is obviously upset."

Mother: Why do you keep struggling with this? Why do you keep challenging yourself? Why do you keep resisting this?

"She's talking about self-love, self-confidence, and self-worth," Staci explained.

Mother: Why can't you love yourself like I love you?

"Andrew, she shows you other lifetimes as your mother, your cousin, in which she served as a guiding presence to you. In at least one of those lives, you were an adult going back home to recover from an experience. She's really exasperated here. Your spirit guide steps forward and places a hand on her shoulder."

Spirit Guide: Be gentle. Be aware that your understanding of the challenge comes from outside the challenge. You cannot understand what it's like from that point of view.

"She didn't realize that she had lapsed into an extreme emotional response. I see her taking a little bit to rebalance and recompose herself."

Mother: In my compassionate love for you, I have chosen to be of service to you through many lifetimes. It is not because I, myself, am perfect. It is because I love you, and through being with you and watching you cope, I learn about me, too, and I learn to control myself better. It may not always look like that because sometimes the learning experience is extreme, and I am not always learning from it in the moment it happens. But, in time I do. Know that I love you.

Andrew: I know this to be true.

Mother: Know that I am always by your side, whether or not I am physically present with you.

Andrew: This I also know to be true.

Mother: When I gave birth to you in our first life [together] . . .

"She is giving a time period I don't recognize," Staci informed us. "It's before recorded history, a civilization that is long gone from Earth."

Mother: . . . I dedicated myself to being a guiding presence and a loving mother to you from then on for the remainder of time. I carried you inside me and felt such a strong connection with you in my heart that I carried this feeling with me wherever I went, near or far, this realm or another. I am aware I become too invested in your good fortune, but know that my intent originates as pure and that what I want for you is always what I consider to be your best.

I may not always know you as well as you might like, because I hold an image in my mind of who you really are and all you are capable of. I must ask that you forgive me when I am too attached to what I think you should be. Forgive me, my son.

Andrew: I do, now and always, forever.

My strength is too often found in you, and I push myself, sometimes stridently, to move on and let go of you. I have done this in other lifetimes, and I may do this again. I am aware that my relationship with you is a delicate one and that I may ask more of you at times than you feel you can give.

Mother: I believe you are capable. I believe in you profoundly. I believe in your ability to heal. I will always encourage resilience in you to further strengthen the great courage you have built within yourself and that goes with you from one life to the next to the next.

Now you are learning to build stamina. You are learning to build strength. I will sometimes challenge you so that you may go within yourself to pull up the strength instead of depending on me needlessly. I only hope I know the right time to do that and do not err in my judgment.

Andrew: I will forgive you.

Mother: When you weep, I will weep. When you mourn, I will mourn. But in the end you must and will go forward without me. You will carry on with your head held high, stronger than you were before you came into this life. You will go through a metamorphosis that will give you a vision of how you can best be in the world and lend your help to it.

I pray to give you strength, whether it be from my heart or my head, with the knowledge I carry within.

I am your greatest champion.

With that, Staci concluded her remarkable glimpse into Andrew's pre-birth planning session. I asked Andrew if there was anything else he would like to ask.

"Yes," he replied. "The main thing seems to be about self-love. Are there any words of advice as to how I could work on self-love?"

"That's a great question," Staci told him. "Let me be quiet and focus on that." After a few moments of silence, Staci announced that her guide would speak through her.

"You chose the karmic lesson of compassionate awareness to be one in which you wanted to make a transformative growth step in this lifetime. You've always been of a compassionate mindset toward others, but you have held it least for yourself. You have lived lives of self-indulgence or self-denial. It is finding the balance between the two—through the use of unconditional love and unwavering compassion for yourself—that brings healing.

"This means that instead of holding on to ideals of how things should have been, which makes you hold on to the disappointment that then creates anger, you are working on accepting and allowing by being more centered and calming your reactions to the things that happen in life, whether they happen to you, for you, or to somebody else.

"Always, always treat yourself as if you were your own child. Love yourself compassionately through your life, so when you make what you think is a mistake or an error in judgment, you are able to then say to yourself, 'That's all right. Maybe that happened this time. It's a learning experience. I still love you, and next time you will do better.'

"Whatever the words you might say, take the attitude that you are your very own child, whom you love with all your heart and soul and whom you would never want to hurt. Love yourself from the ground up. That will foster a more adaptive, loving response to life itself within your heart, within your personal energy.

"There is one more thing," added Staci's guide. "We [Spirit] suggest to you that at the end of your meditations you say, 'I am at peace with the world, myself, and everyone in it.' When we are trying to induce change within ourselves, it is good to say that silently or aloud three or more times. The mind needs something repeated three times in order to 'flip a switch' from being in a place of self-criticism, outside of self-love, to being in a place of compassion and greater capacity to be unconditionally loving of yourself.

"As a holder of the karmic lesson of over-impulsivity, you have to apply yourself to something on a consistent, daily, or near-daily basis over a long period of time to get your desired results. Nothing comes to you very easily or very quickly in this lifetime, because that is the way you set it up. Instead of having short bursts of action to bring about an effect or change, you are learning to persist over a long period of time to create a fundamentally important, foundational change within yourself."

I then asked Staci and her guide if there were any other reasons why Andrew planned the experiences of impotence and low libido.

"There was a time earlier in Andrew's journey as a soul when something happened that scarred his soul," Staci said as Spirit began. "I get a Mediterranean feel to this lifetime, 11th or 12th century. I'm being given an image of Andrew carrying a broad sword and in army dress—strong protective leathers, a metal helmet.

"Andrew has been away for a long time on a journey to a battleground. Now the battle is over and he comes home. The village he came from had been invaded, and many people had been killed. Even though his family had been hidden in a cave in the mountains a short distance from the village, they were still discovered, and he finds that his children and his wife were slaughtered."

Staci's speech slowed as she started again to channel her guide.

"Andrew blamed himself. He took responsibility for the death of his family and felt that he did not deserve another family until he forgave himself. As we know, forgiveness requires compassion and love, so these are things Andrew works on within himself now. Perhaps later in this life, perhaps in another life, he can then allow himself to create children again and to hold the loving family bond.

"Andrew must increase his state of compassionate awareness and self-love to the point where he understands how much he is responsible for and what is beyond the realm of his responsibility, such as unknown unseen invaders killing those he loves.

"Andrew's emotional being sustained a scarring injury in that life, but one that proved Andrew's courageous nature. Andrew submitted himself willingly to a long-term lesson of multiple lives through which he would heal and learn to embrace and love himself unconditionally through the increasing of his compassionate awareness toward himself and all he loves. This generosity of spirit and this courageous nature are Andrew's greatest strengths.

We hope that you [Rob] carry on the theme of how courageous a soul can be to plan such difficult and harsh learning experiences into their lives."

I asked Staci's guide if there are other reasons why a soul would plan to experience low libido or impotence.

"It is always about learning to love the self, to look beyond the outer measures of success or beauty, and to accept the core of the individual as whole and complete. Sometimes a soul will take on low libido because of misusing others in a sexual way in other lifetimes, but this, too, comes down to the foundational lessons of learning to love unconditionally and learning to increase compassionate awareness."

"Why did Andrew plan to experience low libido and impotence as a man and not as a woman?" I wondered.

"Because Andrew enjoys feeling the great strength of his body, which he knew the female form would not carry," Staci's guide answered. "Neither was he ready to engage in the level of emotional complexity the female body houses. This is another reason why Andrew has chosen his neurological system as a physical element requiring balance in his life—because the female form has more neurological tissue than the male. Andrew wanted to learn to balance and handle the male neurological system first."

"Why, then, would someone plan to experience low libido or impotence as a woman?"

"In the case of a woman it is again about unconditional love, but it is also about self-protection—the feeling of having been harmed or fearing harm. It is a way of self-isolating and setting barriers that would enable the individual to increase its relationship with itself by having more time with itself. And for some women—and men as well—the experience houses the concept of self-forgiveness, the need to learn to forgive the self for not living up to certain ideals the personality might hold."

"What more can you say," I asked, "about how to cope with low libido or impotence?"

"Place yourself in the moment of *now*, where your power lies," advised Staci's guide. "Practice being here now instead of some imagined reality. During those times when you're not feeling overwhelmed by it, write a few sentences declaring your love for yourself, declaring how good things are in your life, even if the only thing that's good is that the grass is growing or a bee is buzzing around a flower outside your window. And we suggest the individual make a new habit of declaring 'I love me' on a daily basis."

Abruptly, Staci's speech returned to its faster, normal cadence. "Spirit wants me to share something with you. When I was twenty-five, it was planted in my mind [by Spirit] that every time I passed a mirror I would say either silently or out loud, 'I love me.' It took about twenty-five years [of doing that] until one day out of habit I passed by the mirror and found myself saying 'I LOVE ME' and realized I'd finally gotten there."

"Staci," I asked, "what would your guide say to someone who is struggling as the partner of someone with low libido or impotence?"

"Be kind."

⌒

When not in body and seemingly bound by the limitations of the physical realm and the five senses, Andrew, like each of us, is an infinitely powerful soul. Existing simultaneously in multiple dimensions, he is free of the mirage of time, unrestricted by the illusion of space. Because consciousness is nonlocal in nature, Andrew is active concurrently in numerous physical and non-physical realms. He creates instantly through thought alone. He knows experientially, not just intellectually, his oneness with All That Is.

How powerful must a soul be to hide such power *from itself*? In his current lifetime, Andrew sought to blind himself temporarily to his vast power in part because he used it irresponsibly in a past life. That self-same power is still there but hidden from his view by the cloak of impotence. As his spirit guide Elar told him, "You are blocking yourself from accepting what you already are."

That block dissolves as Andrew forgives himself for his actions in the past life. Self-forgiveness, in turn, blossoms in the writing of letters of self-compassion, self-worth, and self-love to himself. Because giving and receiving are in truth one and the same, the act of writing such letters is the receiving of the gifts they contain.

Yet, there is more to power than simply the ability to conceal one's true nature from oneself. As Elar explained to Andrew, true power is not power over others but rather the ability to draw their innate power *out of them*. That is accomplished through the honest sharing of feelings most seek to avoid: pain, fear, and vulnerability. Great strength is required for Andrew to share his suffering freely and openly. His strength both reminds others of their own and elicits it from them. It is for this reason that Iknow told Andrew, "The doorway to love and transcendence is through fear . . . There they will meet you. There love will be found." On the Earth plane little is as it seems, and much is the opposite. On Earth impotence can be a springboard to a deeper knowing of one's limitless power. In the physical realm, fear can be a touchstone of transcendent love.

Iknow further advises Andrew to "embrace your insecurities . . . [but] not to change or get rid of them." To attempt to rid oneself of anything is to be in a state of resistance. Resistance requires focus, focus lends energy, and energy creates more of the object of one's focus. In truth there is nothing for Andrew to get rid of, only aspects of self to love. Inner alchemy is not a process of selective rejection but rather one of whole-hearted, indiscriminate embrace.

To the extent Andrew learns to love himself unconditionally, he creates Heaven on Earth for himself, or as Iknow put it, he unites "back to the Source that you never left." No soul is ever truly separate from Source or God, but we choose to *perceive* such separation when we incarnate on Earth. As Andrew remembers his great power, he returns Home in his awareness. Here lies much of the service-to-others portion of Andrew's pre-birth blueprint. By experiencing the opposite of who he truly is and then shedding that self-deception, Andrew carves an energetic pathway back to oneness consciousness. "In the returning," Iknow told him, "you can take others with you." Far more powerful than any action he will ever take with his physical body, Andrew's expansion in consciousness helps countless seeming others to follow in his footsteps.

Like so many who incarnate on the Earth plane, Andrew designed a learning-through-opposites life plan. The soul learns best through the experience of opposites, which provide the contrast needed to understand who one really is at the soul level. The starker the contrast, the more profound the potential self-knowing. As Iknow described, "It's like pushing a ball under water. The farther you push it, the farther it's going to spring up." Through the pain of impotence, Andrew is in the process of forging and gifting to himself a deep, rich, substantial, and beautiful self-awareness of his own strength and magnificence.

Before either were born, Sarah agreed to be Andrew's co-teacher in his lessons. Even though they planned for their relationship to be temporary on the level of the personality, their pre-birth discussion makes clear that her love for him is strong and enduring on the level of the soul. Impotence gives Andrew both the opportunity and the motivation to cultivate greater self-love. So, too, does the painful loss of his Earthly relationship with Sarah. She foresaw this opportunity when she told Andrew in their pre-birth planning to "fall in love and be in love with yourself over and over again." This current lifetime is the one in which so many of us hoped and planned before we were born to discover that *we ourselves* are the great love of our lives.

How is such self-love attained? As Staci's guide pointed out, Andrew's impotence leads him to self-protect and self-isolate, which in turn provides an opportunity to increase his relationship with himself. What might that relationship look like? "Always, always treat yourself as if you were your own child," Staci's guide advised Andrew. The spiritual path is one on which each of us realizes that we can and must be our own best friend, guide, healer, and parent. So that he may make this discovery, Andrew's impotence, low libido, and "failed" relationship with Sarah are all intended to turn him back unto himself. As I know wisely told Andrew, "you *are* that end goal."

Andrew's experience of impotence is creating both a profound knowing of who he really is—Love—and a greatly expanded capacity to love. After this lifetime is over, when impotence is but a vague and distant memory, Andrew will carry those ideals with him for all eternity.

This is the path of the spiritual warrior.

CHAPTER 3

Interdimensional Parenting

S OME YEARS AGO THE PUBLISHER of the Spanish editions of my books sent me to Mexico to do a series of promotional interviews on radio and TV. The translator and I were riding in a taxi in Mexico City discussing a wide variety of subjects when she briefly referred to a friend who was engaged in "interdimensional parenting." She said it with complete nonchalance and then quickly went on to another subject.

"Wait a minute," I interrupted. "Did you just say you have a friend who is doing *interdimensional parenting?*"

"Yes." She seemed surprised that this phrase had somehow caught my attention.

"What in the world is *interdimensional parenting?*"

"Well, my friend's husband died. He's now helping her from the other side to raise their child."

This stopped me. We sat in silence for a few moments watching the people flow by as I tried to wrap my mind around what I had just heard.

"Would she be willing to talk with me?" I asked.

"I'll ask."

Not long thereafter I found myself speaking with Alexa Pauls, whose husband, Jorge, is indeed co-parenting their son from the nonphysical realm.

In the United States alone, by the age of fifteen an estimated 1.5 million children lose one or both parents. The number for the rest of the world is surely multiples of that number. The parent who remains in body naturally wonders, "Why did this happen? What does it mean? How can I raise children by myself?" The parent and children often feel abandoned. They may feel anger toward the family member who died and guilt in regard to feeling anger. The wounds from such a loss are deep and long-lasting.

How then does healing take place? Perhaps, just perhaps, through understanding that the "deceased" never really left.

Alexa

Alexa was thirty-nine years old at the time I spoke with her, four years after the death of her husband, Jorge. She was born in Germany, the daughter of a diplomat and a family therapist. She spent the first half of her life moving from country to country with her family. On a post-high-school graduation trip to Mexico, she experienced an inexplicably strong feeling of connection with the archeological sites she visited, even spontaneously bursting into tears in Tulum. She then chose to pursue Precolombian Studies while in college in Berlin. She moved to Mexico after finishing her master's degree. Shortly thereafter she met Jorge, an adventure sports guide and reporter.

"From the first moment I saw Jorge, I was very moved," Alexa said wistfully. "I found him extremely attractive; there was a special spark in his yellow-brown eyes that captured me. At a party Jorge and I talked all night long, immersing ourselves in each other's lives.

Both Alexa and Jorge had other partners at the time they met, but during the next year, as they came to know each other better within their circle of friends, their connection deepened. Alexa remembers a very beautiful dream in which she and Jorge were walking through an arch of clouds, getting married." Soon afterwards they ended their other relationships.

"We had this strong feeling that we had to get together, be together, live together, and walk together on this path of life," Alexa told me. "What followed were eleven years as a couple, very happily living quite a good life, double income, no kids, traveling a lot." Alexa and Jorge shared a love of nature and adventure, spending much of their free time river rafting, mountain climbing, hiking, and exploring remote places.

As the years passed, their thoughts turned toward having children.

"Jorge was a child-loving man," Alexa remembered. "I knew that he really wanted to have children, and we were getting older and older. I was almost thirty-four, and he was forty-four, when I told him, 'OK, let's try before we get too old. Let's see what destiny has prepared for us.' We are certain our son Luca came down to us that very same day—the very first day we tried to conceive. We actually felt how this little soul incarnated in my body. It was a very special moment."

"How did you know?" I asked. "What did it feel like?"

"I felt it not during the lovemaking but right afterward. We were lying in bed, and we looked at each other and said, 'That was different.' Then I closed my eyes, and my inner vision was captured by a vast darkness going beyond the sky to a very far away, dark place. Then I saw light dropping down, making its way through layers of different atmospheres to my abdomen. Then my cat came to our bed, which she never did, climbed up to my abdomen, and started making 'whurrr, whurrr' noises on my tummy. I said, 'Oh, I think somebody arrived.'"

Luca's birth was complicated and required a C-section, but he arrived healthy. "He had huge blue eyes," Alexa recalled, "big ponds in which the sky is reflected. There's a lot of wisdom and depth in those eyes." Alexa and Jorge were blissfully happy.

Not long thereafter Jorge was offered a live TV show presenting adventure sports four days a week. It seemed as though all their dreams had come true.

"When Luca was eleven-and-a-half months old, Jorge went on a trip," Alexa said, sadness suddenly in her voice. "It was Tuesday,

January 15, in 2013. He left our house very early in the morning, gave me a kiss. I was half asleep. I said, 'I'll see you tomorrow evening.' Luca and I went to a park in the afternoon. We stayed in the park until 5:00 and then went home. Half an hour later I received a phone call from Jorge's boss.

"He said, 'I have very bad news. Jorge had a fatal plane accident.' I had Luca in one arm and the telephone in the other hand. 'NO, THIS CAN'T BE POSSIBLE!' I screamed. I fell to the floor. "'NO! NO! WHAT ARE YOU TELLING ME? WHAT ARE YOU TELLING ME?'"

The pilot with whom Jorge had been flying had forty years and 24,000 hours of experience. For fifty minutes all went well as they did various tricks and loops in the air. The error came during the landing. The pilot, who had left his own airplane in another city and was flying the plane of the airport owner, miscalculated—badly. The plane slid into the jungle by the side of the landing strip. The impact killed both the pilot and Jorge.

"If we go back to the moment when I received the phone call," Alexa continued, "I remember leaving my body and traveling to where Jorge was by the site of the accident. I remember flying out to where he was and telling him in a desperate way, *Jorge, this was not supposed to happen! We were supposed to be a happy couple and lead a happy life!*' Instantly I received a clear answer, him telling me, *'Yes, Alexa, this is the way it is supposed to be.*'"

Alexa made some phone calls, and within 30 minutes her house filled with her friends and Jorge's family. "From then on my house was full of people for six days. It was an amazing experience of community: sharing emotions, traditions, companionship. Always, always one of my girlfriends was with me to watch over Luca or go to the bank or cook. I was never alone."

I asked Alexa at what point she came to the concept of inter-dimensional parenting.

"I felt Jorge's presence very strongly during those first nights in the house," she answered. "I once was with Luca in my arms in his room, trying to make him go to sleep. I felt Jorge embrace us. The three of us were a column of light!

"On the second night of bringing Luca to bed, I took the little boy in my arm outside on our terrace. I said, 'Goodnight, trees. Goodnight, stars. Goodnight, sky,' as we usually did—a nightly ritual. And that night I said, 'Goodnight, Papa. He's out there, and he will always watch over you.' Then I carried the little boy into his room. As I was closing the door, Luca looked outside the door and said, 'Bye bye, Papa.' He had never used the word *Papa*. For me it was very clear that he saw his father."

Alexa began to consult Jorge on major decisions. She felt him guide her to move from Mexico City to a small town two hours away. There he led her to a beautiful small replica of the house in which she and Jorge had lived in Mexico City prior to his death, a place where she knew she and Luca would feel safe and at home. "Since he passed away from this physical plane I never stopped talking to him, especially at night. Usually, I would light a candle and create a calm moment to talk with Jorge just as we had done when he was here."

On one of these candlelit nights Alexa asked Jorge why he had left, leaving her with the responsibility of raising their son, what he thought about her way of managing this, and how he saw Luca. As an answer she received the term "interdimensional parenting" *in English* in her mind. She held her breath as she grasped the meaning of this expression she had never heard before. Alexa understood intuitively that the term is of great significance. At one and the same time it both thrilled her and instilled a deep calm.

She then told me that Luca is in contact with Jorge as well.

"Just a few weeks ago Luca said, 'Mama, I will paint everybody who lives in this house.' I was very curious of the outcome of this little drawing because we have various pets and he has a nanny who lives with us as well. So I was prepared for Mama, Luca, the nanny, and the dogs.

"Later he brought me the drawing. It was a house with Luca, Mama, and a round sphere—an egg—standing in the house. It's a very different figure than the more human figures of myself and Luca. It's a stick with two legs and a big, egg-like shape with two eyes and a smile."

Alexa asked Luca what the egg shape is.

"Papa," he answered matter-of-factly.

"Why is Papa different?" she asked, startled.

"I don't know," Luca replied. "That's the way he is."

Luca was seeing his father in the home, apparently in light-body, in a mostly oval shape.

I asked Alexa to tell me about another time she had communicated with Jorge.

"Once, maybe a year ago, I was in a Temazcal, which is a traditional Mexican sweat bath. I somehow connected with Jorge. I saw him sitting on the terrace of our house, trying out the couch and the cushions and enjoying being there. I told him, *'Wow, you're at home!* Enjoy it, because it's also your house because you led us to this house.' The next thing I saw was him standing in Luca's bedroom with Luca asleep in his bed. It was very moving because I sensed that he was desperate to touch his son but wasn't able. I said, 'I'm so sorry you can't enjoy him in a clearer way, but that's your son, and I know you are there to watch over him.' Then I saw him sitting on the floor before the front of the bed, watching over Luca."

Alexa then shared a special dream in which Jorge had come to her.

"I was flying through the sky, travelling through vast darkness. All of the sudden I was right next to the image of the Sistine Chapel of God and Adam [extending their arms and index fingers to touch each other]. I saw and felt their fingers getting closer and closer. At the moment when the fingers touched, there was a big boom, a lot of light, an explosion! In the same second I saw one of those old photograph booths with a curtain floating [in front of it]. I stepped forward to open that curtain . . . and saw Jorge! He was sitting in the booth. He stood up. He was brilliant, beautiful . . . *more beautiful than ever.* It was him: his body, his eyes, his hair, and everything in a very shiny presentation of him. It was the true, essential Jorge. He still exists, and he exists in a shinier version of himself than the one I knew on Earth," Alexa added with a laugh.

"It's like the Sistine Chapel image of the two fingers represents interdimensional contact," I observed.

"Exactly," she agreed.

In addition to her own communications with Jorge, Alexa received a message from him through a friend who reads the Akashic Records, the complete, nonphysical record of every thought, word, and action relevant to the Earth plane. Alexa read Jorge's words to me:

Hello Loved One,

I'm Jorge. I'm always here with you, and I'm very happy and relieved that you know I am. I am always present. Please don't stop communicating with me. Please believe in the fact that this [interdimensional parenting] is possible and actually happening. You know that. Your soul knows it. You know this is happening.

I had to 'pass away' so that you started believing in the existence of other realities. Believe in your intuition.

Luca's soul is very ancient and wise. We have to take care of him. I am always close to you. I communicate through telepathy in the day and also dreams at night. I never went away. You know it. Your soul knows. I appreciate and am profoundly thankful for your service, altruism, and the truths you express in your acts of love. You have to learn to believe without doubting yourself. In prior lives you suffered a lot because of your abilities, but that time is now over, and consciousness is opening up. You have to wake up and stay awake. You are doing it very well with Luca—very well, and this little one is our biggest teacher. He is of an ancient lineage full of knowledge. When he grows up, we will see this.

You are a soul in service, and we [Spirit] are thankful for your work. We know it's not easy, but you can do it. Remember that your soul decided all this would happen and that you have the strength and the love of your son that makes it possible to go through this. You are going to do very well, my loved one. Love and don't look backward, because you are doing very well. Your book will come out. Many souls are waiting for it.

You are very loved, my beautiful princess.

We were silent for a minute as we took in the power and beauty of Jorge's words.

"Alexa," I said, "did the concept of interdimensional parenting help you to heal any anger you felt toward Jorge and forgive him?"

"Oh, yes. The clear perception that it was supposed to be that way helped me tremendously. Obviously, there were days when I thought, *I don't want to get up. I just want to be depressed and lie in bed*, but that was not possible because I had to take care of my little son. So, the understanding that we ourselves had planned that, in combination with taking care of a light, beautiful, joyous baby boy, was my medicine to get through these difficult first years."

"Your story will be read by people who have lost their spouses and are raising one or more children seemingly alone. This may be their first exposure to the idea of interdimensional parenting. Perhaps they've been angry with their partner for quite some time for seemingly leaving them. What would you say to those people?"

"Instead of feeling victimized, alone, depressed, and powerless, it's better to really get into these challenges and through them in an intense way," she advised. "Grieve in an intense way. Cry in an intense way. Flow in an intense way, but without falling. Look through that curtain of grief and see the potential. Be thankful for the opportunity to understand what it means to be here with or without body."

"Alexa, some people who read your story may be children who are old enough to understand the concept of interdimensional parenting and who have lost one of their parents. What do you want to say to them?"

"Whenever you feel their presence, believe in that, hold on to that, and find relief and love in those moments. I believe that both nighttime and nature are places where it is a lot easier to connect. So, I recommend that the children think at night about their parent and invoke them. I always tell Luca, 'Your father loves you. Your father watches over you,' every, every night. The parent can explain to these children in a playful—not a spiritual or indoctrinating way—that 'In your dreams you are able to fly. You can go to the stars. Maybe your mother or father will come and pick you up and take you on a ride.'

"And also connect through nature. Every week in many different moments I say, 'Look at the bird, the light in the tree, [or hear] the wind. Your father is there.' Go to the woods and talk to them in nature, and don't ever stop talking to them.

"Tell your [transitioned] mother or father what you did in school. Tell them what worries you, or if somebody did something that you didn't like. Tell your parent about it, and you will feel that they are there, that they can take care of you and help you and be by your side."

I asked Alexa to summarize how interdimensional parenting helps her, Luca, and Jorge.

"It helps myself because I don't feel alone," she said. "I've felt sad. I've longed for him physically. But I haven't felt alone. I feel very strong and certain to walk on because I feel his companionship.

"For Luca, in his day-to-day life Jorge's definitely present. Somehow Luca does not give the impression of being a boy of just a single mom, longing for some missing part. I believe that a big part of all this is directed toward raising Luca with a consciousness of a multidimensional world and existence, preparing him from baby times onward that we don't live only on this physical plane. As an adult and a man, this will play an important role in his life and mission.

"Creating consciousness around this concept will make it a lot easier for Jorge to play a role in Luca's life. Luca will have a very special guide. I think a lot of the significance we will discover in the future."

"Alexa, is there anything else you'd like to say to children who have lost a parent, maybe even those who are now adults and had one parent pass away when they were young?"

"I'd like to tell the children that the spirit of their passed-away mother or father can incarnate in a bird or a river of water, or that they can encounter them in little, magical signs. Once you open up and start reading these signs, they make your life magical and beautiful. Even for the older, already-adult people who lived through the experience a long time ago, it will never be too late to connect to the presence of the soul because time is so different in the spirit world. They can always connect to the presence of their parent, who has certainly never left them."

Speaking with Jeshua and Jorge

My conversation with Alexa had left me with many questions. Had she, Jorge, and Luca all agreed before they were born that Jorge would return to Spirit shortly after Luca's birth? If so, why had Alexa wanted to raise Luca alone? Why had Luca wanted to be raised by only his mother? If these had been their pre-birth intentions, why had Jorge agreed to their plan? To learn the answers to these and other questions about their life blueprints, I asked Pamela to channel both Jeshua and Jorge.

To begin our exploration, I asked Jeshua to provide a definition of interdimensional parenting.

"Interdimensional parenting means there is a loving relationship between a parent who has left the physical realm and a child still in the physical realm. The relationship is characterized by care, commitment, and support from the parent. The parent is assisted by at least two guides to perform their function from the other side. Fulfilling this role is part of their soul's plan for inner growth.

"It is necessary that the [deceased] parent be able to connect with their own soul or higher self. There must be a level of awareness in the parent that enables them to rise above the strong emotions they have about the child: concern, grief, anger, or fear about losing the child or about their own death. This transpersonal [soul-level] awareness makes sure that the child—and the remaining partner on Earth if there is one—really benefits from this interdimensional relationship. And it helps the deceased parent to come to terms with their own emotions, because the soul's perspective provides a larger picture.

"Interdimensional parenting is almost always part of the soul plan of the people involved. This means it will very likely happen, that it belongs to the category of events in life that have a high probability because the souls have chosen beforehand to experience it."

Pamela jumped in to clarify. "As opposed to situations in which the parent dies and cannot let go of the Earth realm and their child (and so remains Earth-bound), and the relationship is more characterized by heavy emotions of loss and sadness, interdimensional parenting does not happen from the astral (Earth-bound) realm, but from the spiritual realm, where there is a substantial level of freedom and awareness."

Jeshua then stepped aside so Pamela could offer her initial impressions of Jorge, who had been waiting quietly to participate.

"I see Jorge," Pamela said. "He looks like in the picture [Alexa had sent to her] but is dressed in white clothes with dark stripes at the wrists and ankles and black boots that look very earthly." [Jorge could have presented to Pamela in any form of his choice, including as just light. He had chosen an appearance familiar to Pamela and by extension Alexa to create feelings of connection and comfort.] "He is weeping. His heart is full of love for his wife and child. He still yearns to be with them, to hold them and caress them. He still has very human emotions about this. But, he is also in a place of light and very pure, peaceful energy. He wants to say **I love you** to Alexa and Luca and that he will be there when they cross over. He is clearly very committed to them. He also says he is proud of them, about the way they are coping. He says they are warriors of consciousness, creating more light on Earth as they pursue their individual paths of growth.

"Jorge likes to cooperate with this book, because he says that there is a category of deceased parents who *could be* involved in interdimensional parenting but who are now stuck in the astral dimension, where they suffer from heartbreak and loss. There are some whose soul's plan it is to be an interdimensional parent but who still feel too much stuck in heavy emotions to rise to the transpersonal level. He wants to speed up the process of liberation by providing information to the ones left behind on Earth. Those people can talk to their loved ones, which would help the loved ones a lot. People in the astral realm can often be reached more easily by physical people on Earth than by their guides because they don't acknowledge their guides yet.

"There are also," Pamela continued, "deceased parents who do not have a soul plan to be an interdimensional parent but who could still become one if they sincerely want it. It could help them grow, let go, and understand a lot of things. They may not become a 'full-fledged interdimensional parent' but more like a 'trainee.' Jorge stresses that there is a lot of free choice in the universe. There are some basic tendencies in a soul plan, but there is a lot of leeway, too. So, you can have the soul plan to become an interdimensional parent but not make it for quite some time because you get stuck in heavy emotions. You can also not have this plan but still evolve into an interdimensional parent because you choose to open to the soul level and are eager to liberate yourself from the more dense astral realm. *You can plan events, but you cannot plan spiritual growth. The latter involves free choice.*

"Jorge says that more awareness in our human society about life on the other side and what it is like there for a parent crossing over could enhance the interdimensional communication and help both groups of souls."

"Pamela," I asked, "did Alexa plan before she was born to 'lose' Jorge and then engage in interdimensional parenting, and if so, why?"

"Alexa and Jorge have a very strong bond, and they were together before, in several lifetimes," Pamela answered. Here she was using her gifts of clairvoyance ("clear seeing"), claircognizance ("clear knowing"), and clairsentience ("clear feeling") to access information about both their past lives and what their energies were like in those incarnations. "He was her father in one life, and they both had trouble letting each other go when she became mature. She always compared the men she met with him, and they always fell short. She became judgmental of them and didn't open to them.

"There were other past life relationships, too—she being his mother. They were devoted to each other in a similar way.

"There's one lifetime where they are both male, good friends and companions. They have a lot of fun together; they are both adventurous, passionate, and daring. I see them riding horses together full speed with some other men in an open landscape. Maybe they are tradesmen traveling around. It's exhilarating, and they love this life of freedom. They look a bit down on people who are more careful, narrow-minded, or stuck in restrictive ways of thinking.

"Jorge and Alexa have similar temperaments in all their lifetimes. Both are spirited, daring, and adventurous. There was always deep fondness for each other, but so much so that it hampered their relationship with other people," Pamela concluded.

Jeshua then returned to the forefront of Pamela's consciousness. "The bond has been too strong in some ways," he observed. "There is a need to disentangle and become whole unto themselves. Jorge's early death was part of Alexa's soul plan because she wanted to learn to cope with the loss and manage on her own. She wanted to develop the qualities of patience, trust, and surrender as she goes through the mourning process. At the same time, she has a very adventurous spirit and wanted to be consciously involved in interdimensional parenting, like a pioneer. The strong bond between her and Jorge makes this possible. So, she wants to overcome the disadvantage of the relationship (attraction so strong that it shuts out other people and slows down progress), but she does so in a way that uses the positive side of it: the strong soul-level connection. The soul connection can help her still feel the love between Jorge and her and create the space for a high level of interdimensional interaction, but at the same time she is on her own at the human level and has to cope emotionally."

"But isn't that sense of oneness that Jorge and Alexa have experienced together love?" Pamela asked him. "What's wrong with that?"

"It isn't wrong as much as it is one-sided," Jeshua explained. "There's a level of excitement and brashness in both their energies that is reinforced by being together. The result can be a lack of patience, surrender, and equanimity. They need opposite energies more than they need each other now. However, the relationship as it is now (outside the flesh) fosters the qualities of patience and surrender. So, in a very creative way, they have found a way of being together that matches both their soul's purposes."

"That sounds beautiful and even ingenious," Pamela observed, "but I can imagine that Alexa cannot see it like that so easily. She must experience a huge gap in her life now that Jorge is physically absent. Isn't it almost impossible to look at this situation from the soul's perspective when you are in a human body, dealing with intense emotions of grief and loss, in a world that is very focused on the physical and less on the spiritual? If you feel emotionally traumatized, the soul's perspective often seems too lofty. How can you open up to that level of seeing things?"

"You do not open up to your soul's perspective all at once," stated Jeshua. "Usually it takes quite some time to go through the transformational process of dealing with your emotions and opening up to a perspective from which events and situations become meaningful and bear fruit. This is not something you can grasp with your mind alone. Understanding things from the level of your soul is a slow ascension process in which you start by accepting your emotional pain, caring for yourself gently and diligently. The self-love you develop will at some point enable you to reach moments of peace and surrender. The pain is still there, but you do not fight it anymore. You allow it, and this is when true transformation takes place.

"By allowing it to be inside of you, not interfering, you trust at a basic level that it makes some sense, even if you do not understand how. And the next step is that you realize you are bigger than the pain because you are the one allowing it. This is when your consciousness becomes very close to the soul level. If you can stay in that place of surrender and awareness long enough, you'll get glimpses of the possible meaning behind the events that occurred. They pop up in your mind intuitively, like sudden insights that you did not acquire through thinking but through being open and unknowing. It takes courage to surrender to not-knowing, not-understanding, and just being with the pain. But, this creates the entrance to true knowing, not by the mind but by the heart."

"So, the key is acceptance of the pain," Pamela summarized. "But how can you accept pain if it feels unbearable? How can you accept it if you feel like *being* the pain instead of *watching* it?"

"Then you need to accept that it is unbearable right now," Jeshua advised. "Go *with* the flow of your feelings, not against it. If you feel it is unbearable, accept that this is your truth right now. Accept that *right now* the situation is unacceptable to you. Don't fight the pain or the thought that it is unbearable. It's the resistance that creates the biggest impediment to change.

"Note that I said accept how you feel *right now*. Your feelings always change, no matter what the situation is. So, if I say, 'accept that it is unbearable,' I mean 'accept that it is unbearable *now*.' This very acceptance will enhance the possibility that you will feel differently some moments or some days later. 'Accept' always means *accept for now*. Just surrender for this one moment and release the tension of resisting. Then see what happens."

More about Alexa and Jorge's Pre-birth Intentions

"Jeshua, can you tell us more about why Alexa wanted to be involved in interdimensional parenting?" I asked.

"She wants to develop her ability to open her heart to communications with 'the other side,' the realm beyond the physical, especially to grow the trust and surrender this requires," he replied. "She needs to open her sensitive, feminine side to feel aligned with Jorge on a soul level and to let go of the male energy inside her that is sometimes controlling and wanting to take charge rather than trusting and letting go."

I then asked if Jorge had planned before he was born to return to Spirit at a young age and parent from the other side, and if so, why.

"Yes, he did," Jeshua confirmed. "Jorge had a clear plan for this lifetime. He wanted to come back and meet Alexa again, and he wanted to be Luca's father. He knew both from previous lifetimes. In one Luca was a priest, a very calm person with a lot of patience. He was introverted and lived a quiet life in a monastery, not caring much about success or other people's opinions. Jorge came to visit him often. He was a passionate young man with a revolutionary spirit, one who resented the injustices (poverty, inequality, power abuse by authorities) he noticed all around him in society. He was looking for a spiritual understanding of the way things were. That is why he came to Luca. Luca liked him a lot. He liked his passionate nature. Jorge admired and appreciated Luca because he seemed not to care about anything external and had something mysterious and wise about him. Luca was a bit lonely, though, and he loved having Jorge around.

"Jorge wanted to meet with Luca again in this lifetime because there was a lot of love between them and because he knew Alexa would be supported by Luca's soul energy. Alexa benefits from Luca's energy because it is opposite to hers. Luca has the patience and calmness that she wants to develop herself.

"Jorge and Alexa," he continued, "are on the other hand able to provide Luca with the warmth and vitality that was somewhat missing in him in the past life. They help him become proud of himself and self-aware, so that he will be strong enough to express his spiritual energy, his wisdom, in today's world. Luca's soul needs to learn to trust people, to trust that his energy is welcome and much needed in this world. He needs to let go of the high level of introversion he had and participate in this world."

With that, Jeshua stepped aside, and Jorge returned to Pamela's consciousness to offer his thoughts.

"I had to die young," Jorge told us, "because of another life in which I killed people who belonged to a group we were opposed to. I was part of a revolutionary band that wanted to change politics. In the process of spreading our revolutionary ideas, we got very much carried away, and we did not shun violence. The worst thing I did was that I killed an innocent man who begged for his life because he had young children. He wasn't even a bad man; he was just afraid of the authorities and did not dare to stand up to them. I had no compassion and decided to kill him. You were either for or against us was the way I saw it—very short-sighted. My soul wanted to make amends for this and experience firsthand what it's like to be ripped away from a wife and young child. It was a terrible experience, but because it was part of my soul plan, after my physical death I could sense after a while that there was a kind of justification behind it. I worked through the emotional trauma relatively easily with the help of some extremely loving and wise guides."

"So, the early death was not caused only by the desire to change the dynamics between you and Alexa?" I wondered.

"No, there was some personal karma involved, too. It was a mixture of motives."

"Did Alexa agree on the soul level with your early death?"

"Yes, she did. There was a very deep understanding between her and me when we were both still on the other side. We both agreed it was a sacrifice we would make, that it would cause us a lot of grief, but that there was a lot to gain as well, which made it valuable for all three of us."

"Jorge, why did you want to be involved in interdimensional parenting?"

"My guides invited me to do so before I started this life. They pointed at this possibility for me. It felt joyous to me at that time, but I didn't realize fully what it meant yet. I now realize how special and precious it is. I am in Luca's energy field constantly. When you have a child on Earth, there's an invisible energy chord between the parents and the child when it is young. Especially between the mother and the child, but if the dad is involved, he has it, too. You are in touch with the child, sensing where it is and what it needs. There is a kind of alertness in your aware-ness, like an invisible bond that connects you to the child. This energy chord—which I am sure parents recognize from their own experience—is still intact between Luca and me. It is always in the background of my awareness, even if I do other things here on my side of life. For instance, if I travel with my guides and learn about other places and realms in the universe, I am always involved with Luca, sometimes in a less focused way and sometimes very focused. I sense when he needs my energy. When there is fear, insecurity, sadness, or another strong emotion inside him, I am with him in 'no time.' Time is very different here.

"I am able to offer love and support to Luca," he continued, "and provide him with the male energy that a father should offer to his son. It is ironic that I may be able to support him better now that I am on the other side because I see things more clearly from this level of light and understanding. But of course, on the other hand, the direct connection of speaking and looking him in the eyes is missing. However, he is a sensitive boy, and in his heart he senses me and knows I am there. I just hope his mind will stay open to this possibility when he grows up.

"I now see that interdimensional parenting as you call it is helpful to my soul's growth, because I get to understand what real love is about: not interfering, being patient, respecting free choice, and trusting the wisdom in life. The love I have now for Alexa and Luca is very pure, even though it is still mixed with sadness and grief because I cannot be with them physically. Though it still hurts me a lot, I do feel the grief will eventually be my teacher, molding me in such a way that I will become more balanced and in touch with my soul."

Jorge then stepped aside, and Jeshua returned to speak further with us.

"Jeshua," I asked, "did Luca plan before he was born to 'lose' his father early in his life and then be parented by his mother in body and his father from the other side, and if so, why?"

"Yes, he did," Jeshua stated. "He wanted to cooperate with the soul plans of Alexa and Jorge. He loves Jorge and feels connected with him on the soul level. This connection was based on the friendship they had when Luca was a priest in the past life. Luca wanted to help Jorge achieve the purpose behind his soul plan, and he knew he would be able to deal with his father's loss even though it would be difficult at times. Luca is presently affected by his mother's grief, but deep down inside he knows his father is still there for him. It is important for Alexa to recognize his soul's greatness and not see him as a victim of a terrible fate. He can deal with this, and he will grow up to be a sensitive boy who is wise beyond his age. Luca chose this path because he loves Jorge and carries his energy imprint in both his genes and energy field. This he wanted to experience, as much as he wanted also to experience having Alexa as his mother. The flamboyant, exuberant energies of both parents give him what he seeks and what benefits him on the soul level."

"Does Luca know Alexa from a past life?" I wondered.

"Briefly," answered Jeshua. "He came to Alexa in a past life when she became pregnant with his essence in female form. The pregnancy ended prematurely as a miscarriage. They never knew each other very well in earthly terms, but their souls touched during that brief time together. The purpose was to exchange energies and grow because of it. Both were very sad about the early parting, and this left the seed for another meeting (in this life)."

Other Reasons for Interdimensional Parenting

I asked Jeshua if there are other reasons why a soul would plan to have children, then "lose" his or her partner, and then team up with the partner in interdimensional parenting.

"Losing your partner at an early age is a profound experience that shakes a person to the bone, especially when there are children involved," he responded. "There may be various reasons for going through this experience related to past lives and the soul's purpose for this lifetime. You need to take a deeper look at the individual story to get a clear understanding of the web of causes.

"The reasons for getting involved in interdimensional parenting are also various, but I can name a few for the parent staying on Earth:

1. To help your child. The deceased parent can offer a kind of guidance that is helpful because it comes from a larger perspective

based on love, whereas much parenting on Earth is still based on fear and worry.

2. To ease your own suffering, because it is very reassuring and comforting to still feel and sense your partner and be able to communicate together. The communication will not be there all the time, and you will doubt if it is true (because you are human), but the flashes of love and information coming through can really help ease your pain.

3. To learn to trust your inner voice, to connect to the heart and go with your intuition.

4. To reach out to another dimension of reality beyond Earth. As you do so, you become aware of your soul's reality and you open to a deep level of love and understanding, deeper than can be provided by the mind or by the (often narrow) beliefs of society.

5. To become a bridge between this world and the world of the afterlife and to develop your abilities as a channel and medium, which may be applied in other areas of your life, also (helping other people with this ability).

6. To enlarge awareness in society about the afterlife and soul-to-soul communication with deceased loved ones."

I asked, "What are some other reasons why a soul would plan to lose a parent early in life and then be raised by one parent in body and one from the other side?"

"If it is primarily the remaining parent's plan to lose the partner and go through that experience, the child's soul may want to be there to help the living parent, to comfort and support them," Jeshua answered. "There may be a past life involvement that has created love in the child's soul for the living parent, and the soul may want to express it in this way. The child's presence may be an important factor for the remaining parent to keep going and to find a reason for living.

"Another reason may be to develop inner qualities such as maturity, courage, empathy, and stamina at an early age. Often, children choosing this want to deal with certain issues at a young age because they really want to make headway. Losing the parent young will set them apart from their peers, forcing them to go into deep emotional waters early on. Even though it can be very hard, the wisdom and life experience gained will often affect their life paths positively, according to each soul's standards. When a child is raised by a parent who is in conscious contact with the deceased parent, this will offer the child a much wider perspective than usual, and it will enable the child to become familiar with a deep level of love and grace. If the child feels the parent, the child will often have strong intuitive abilities and will apply them later in their environment or in relationships with others.

"Sometimes the soul wants to be a bridge between the living and the deceased parent. In some cases the child is more sensitive to the presence of the deceased parent and can open the living parent's heart and mind to communicate. The child may have intuitive impressions, sightings, or feel/sense messages from the parent. If the living parent is open to it, he or she may start to receive messages and signals, too. So, in that way the child can initiate the connection between the two parents."

"Jeshua, if someone's partner has died, how does that person know if the partner is helping to raise the child?" I asked.

"Essentially, you know this by feeling the partner around, sensing their presence, and feeling reassured, encouraged, and supported. Now, in many people there is doubt about their ability to sense energies or presences beyond the physical. You are trained to become skeptical about that. Your school system does not recognize intuition as a valuable source of information and trivializes it as 'mere imagination.' So, for most parents the greatest challenge is to trust their intuition and rely on the information coming through.

"I am going to make a distinction here between emotion and intuition that can be helpful. There is a difference between wanting, craving, yearning, wishing your partner to be with you on the one hand, and sensing they are there on the other hand. In the first case, you are not peaceful inside. You are in deep pain, and you cry out. You miss your partner, and you feel empty and lonely inside. In this condition it is actually very hard to get in touch. The emotion blocks you from sensing the level of love and oneness at which you can meet your loved one. The emotion itself is understandable and unavoidable for some time.

"When you sense the presence of your partner, it is not like an emotion. It is accompanied by a deep quietness, a stillness. You feel lifted into a higher vibration, even if only briefly. A glimpse of light, hope, and reassurance touches your heart. You feel relieved, like a burden is lifted from your shoulders. You feel joy, even if mixed with sadness. If you have any of these sensations, you know you are being touched by your partner at the soul level.

"You can recognize if the partner is there to help you with raising your child if you often get the sense of their being around in a loving and light way when you are dealing with issues concerning the child. When you worry or doubt what to do, you may suddenly sense there's a different angle of looking at things, or you just feel that things will turn out right anyway. You may not actually sense your partner saying anything, but these uplifting energies come from them.

"Also," Jeshua continued, "observe your child and ask—casually, without pushing—if they feel anything, have had dreams about their dad or mom, or feel a connection with them. The child may be more intuitive (less spoiled by the education system) than you. You can encourage the child to speak about their sensations and let them know it is normal to be in touch with a soul beyond the physical.

"The next step is to trust your feelings. If you feel your partner is near or sometimes think of them strongly without a reason, just greet them from your heart; acknowledge them. Ask if there's anything they want you to know, and just wait. Do not expect the answer to be verbal necessarily; perhaps it will come to you as a feeling or a sudden flash of insight later that day. To connect with the deceased, you must become familiar with a different kind of communication: through images, feelings, sudden realizations.

"It's best to keep the interaction short, light, and playful. If you start to push for answers, your mind will interfere, and you will end up disappointed because you will think you made it up.

The mind is not able to receive this subtle kind of information. *You must work through the feeling center: your heart.* The mind can help to bring the information down and put it into words, but the actual sensing of the energy happens on a different level. It is not the thinking level. It is not the emotional level. It is the level of intuition, the level of 'quietly sensing' or 'just knowing.'

"In general," Jeshua concluded, "your society would benefit enormously if the level of the heart and the intuition would be recognized as a real and valuable source of information. You do not need to be psychic to connect with dead loved ones. It is possible for all people to have heart-to-heart communication with their loved ones in a simple, clear way, if only you were taught how and if the dominant forces in society were more open-minded about this type of communication. If you trust your intuition and do not give in to the overly skeptical voices in your head, you actually help change collective awareness and create space for the level of the heart to be recognized again."

"Jeshua," I said, "some people who read this chapter may feel, after thinking about your words, that they are not engaged in interdimensional parenting, that their partner is truly gone, and that they are all alone in raising their children. What can you say to provide comfort, healing, and understanding that whatever is happening is for the highest good of all concerned?"

"First, no one you love is ever truly gone," he answered. "Love is the greatest power in the universe, and whenever you have loved someone, you will be connected to them, whether they are living on Earth or elsewhere. The laws of time and space and of birth and death cannot keep souls apart, ever. It is essential you realize that. It is only when you feel separated from the unifying power of love, when you feel lonely and worn out, that it may seem you are all alone. But, you are not. Even if your deceased partner is not involved in co-parenting the child, there will be highly evolved and loving guides right beside you.

"Especially when you are going through a crisis, an intense mourning process, the assistance from the other side is multiplied and you are showered with love and grace. You may think

'I don't feel anything,' but I have to say that it is you closing the door to it. The help *is* available. It is very understandable that you become temporarily closed off from love and help, because if you feel traumatized by something, in this case the early death of your partner, you resist what happened and cannot accept it. The non-acceptance tells you that whatever happened cannot have happened for good reasons. It feels wrong, and you are not going to let that idea go for a while. This is the most difficult phase in any mourning process. It's not the grief alone, but the added resistance to what's happening to you, that makes it hard to bear.

"I want to say," he added, "that for a single parent who lost their partner, the amount of love and support available to you is *the same* whether your partner is involved in parenting your child from the other side or not."

"Why would the parent on the other side not be involved?" I wondered.

"There may be several reasons," Jeshua replied. "First, they need to focus more on their own emotional healing and/or unresolved issues and are guided to go on an inner journey of awakening on the other side. Their heart will still be connected with you and your child; that bond is eternal. But they will not be involved on the level of everyday life in the way an interdimensional parent is.

"Second, they may be called to enter another incarnation because this may serve their soul's purpose best. Again, this does not mean the connection is broken, because on the soul level an incarnation is like one beam of light coming out of the sun (the soul), flowing down into a particular portion of space-time on Earth. The soul is still present and available for the parent and child remaining on Earth, but the involvement is at a higher level, which may feel like it is more distant. Essentially, however, it is still love.

"Third, for several reasons it may not be your and their soul agreement to be involved in interdimensional parenting. These reasons need not be negative at all; it is about choices being made. If your deceased partner is not involved in co-parenting the child with you, it is not a sign of failure. It does not mean there is something wrong or that someone did something wrong. Please don't look at it this way. The intricate web of relations between souls and events in the universe is far more subtle and profound than such a simple judgment would allow. You can be sure that you get the kind of help you need and that fits your circumstances best."

Having relayed all my questions to Jeshua and his answers to me, Pamela then resumed her own questioning.

"Does it happen," she asked, "that a parent is involved in inter-dimensional parenting and that the partner and child on Earth are completely unaware of it? Can the parenting from the other side still work and be effective in that situation?"

"Yes, it can," Jeshua replied. "This does happen, and if it does, the parent and child on Earth do receive messages and healing energies, but they do not experience them consciously. But, you can receive energy from the other side without knowing it, and it can still affect you positively."

"Because this is essentially what happens in the relationship between a human being and the personal guides, right?" Pamela asked. "Most people are unaware of their guides, but there still is a 'working relationship,' isn't there?"

"Exactly."

"But, does that mean people can be influenced against their will by their guides or by their deceased partners?"

Jeshua clarified. "It is more subtle than that. All human beings have free choice and create their own reality. What you deeply believe to be true will create a range of experiences for you. If a guide and anyone else offer you something that goes against a very deep-seated belief in you, they will not get through to you. So, if you are convinced that you are unworthy, their love may not reach you entirely. However, people are multi-layered beings. You may be bitter and desperate at a conscious level but still have a deep, 'irrational' sense of hope and faith inside. Spiritual guides or deceased loved ones can access that deeper layer and infuse it with the energy of hope and trust, *reinforcing what is already there*. That is what interdimensional parents will do when loved ones on Earth do not respond consciously to them. They will reinforce the seeds of light that are already slumbering inside you, thereby making them more accessible to your everyday awareness as soon as you choose that."

"So basically," Pamela summarized, "you never know for sure if your deceased partner is *not* present with you co-parenting your child, because if you don't sense them, they may still be there without your knowing it."

"Yes, that's true," Jeshua confirmed. "But don't make a problem out of that. There are two possibilities. Either you have clear feelings and intuitions about your partner, in which case there is a conscious connection, or you don't, in which case they may still be involved in interdimensional parenting.

"It is not always necessary that you become involved in conscious communication. Ask yourself: Do I feel drawn to exploring this for myself? Do I feel like developing my intuitive skills, perhaps learning more about sensing energies and communicating with the other side? Follow your natural inspiration and sense of what is right for you. Again, if your partner is involved from the other side and you are not aware of it consciously, it is not a sign you are failing or doing something wrong. For some it will indeed be beneficial and joyful to develop their intuitive communication skills. But if you don't feel up to it or if it does not appeal to you so much, there will be other ways in which you benefit from the connection. You can work directly on letting go of fear-based beliefs or simply focus on loving and nurturing yourself more. In that way the positive energies of your partner will get to you at levels outside of waking consciousness."

With that, Pamela said, Jeshua stepped back and Jorge came forward once more.

"Jorge," I asked, "what else can you say to help people who have lost their partners and who are seemingly raising children alone to understand the deeper spiritual meaning and purpose of interdimensional parenting?"

"The relationship between lovers who are separated by the physical boundary of death can still be very deep and rewarding," Jorge answered. "It is entirely different from sharing your life physically with someone. Because of the physical absence, the emphasis naturally shifts to the soul level, which is the most essential level. The same goes for the relationship with the child. The love relationship between the two partners and between the deceased partner and the child still evolves and grows, and all involved can grow at a higher speed because of the deep and intense feelings involved."

I asked Jorge to share some specific times he helped Alexa raise Luca from the other side.

"I am helping both Alexa and Luca in different ways. I often approach Luca with much warmth and joy. I want to support him to keep his heart open and not absorb Alexa's grief too much. Children live more in the Now and can deal with the mourning process in a lighter way. Sensitive children, however, can pick up the remaining parent's sadness quite deeply. I am trying to prevent this for Luca by letting him know I am alive and sending him joy.

"I play with Luca when he is dreaming at night, just like a father and son would do in the physical realm. We have fun together. For a moment we feel the carelessness of just having a good time and not thinking of the future. This moves me a lot and is healing to my soul as well.

"I am with Alexa often. I stand behind her in my energy body. I envelop her with my love and care and send warm energy into her shoulders, back, and chest. I connect with her heart-to-heart from the middle of my chest to hers. Sometimes I feel resistance in her because she is upset and loses faith. I understand this. It is human.

"I try to encourage Alexa with regard to Luca and energetically make her feel she can trust him and his own strength and gifts. She would feel better if she worried less and would let go of needing to control things. 'Please do not see Luca as a victim,' I say to her. He is strong and powerful and able to become the radiant star he is inside, despite losing his father so young. He can make it."

"Jorge, how can Alexa know if you're telling her something? How can she consciously make contact with you?"

"Alexa, trust your feelings. You have a powerful intuition; trust it again. Feel the grief and the anger and the resistance, too. It is okay. It is part of life and part of the process. But, in very quiet moments when you are tired and weary of these emotions, become very still and hear the whispers of your heart. Your heart will speak to you and tell you what to do. A new path will unfold for you and Luca, and I will be there right beside you to support both of you. How do you know when I am with you? You can recognize it by the feelings you have. If you feel hope again, if you can see things from a lighter perspective, when you feel less heavy and sad, this is when our communication channel is open."

Jeshua then stepped forward to add to Jorge's wisdom.

"The key in communicating with a deceased loved one is to find a quiet space within, where you are neither in your mind nor very emotional. This is where intuition resides. This is a natural place to be that does not require being psychic. What is helpful to find this inner space is to spend time alone in nature or in a place that soothes you and to start to feel comfortable with yourself and your emotions. It is only after you face your emotions and accept them that you can reach a state of peace and surrender. This is the state in which your heart opens to receive messages from the beyond."

Pamela then offered her thoughts for Alexa.

"Go with the flow of the heavy emotions," she advised. "Do not suppress them; they need to be experienced. But every emotion ends at some point, and then there is a moment of silence in which you surrender because you are exhausted. This is the moment where Jorge can reach you. He wants to send you love first and foremost. For you it's important to just bask in that love for a while before you ask questions. Just feel him, so you get used to how he feels now. When that foundation is created, you can start to ask short questions, or you can ask him to give you just one clear message. It is important to let this communication evolve from the feeling level and not jump in with your mind too quickly.

"Also, see Jorge as a human being. He is not all-knowing just because he is on the other side. He certainly has a much wider perspective and more knowledge available, but he is still the human being you knew on Earth. Talk to him like that—as a friend and partner—and sometimes ask how you can help *him*, because he is still struggling, too.

Pamela concluded: "Despite the overwhelming sadness, remember the good times and cherish them in your heart. You will find that you can still have fun together when you connect from the other side; you may laugh out loud when you make jokes or share funny stories. When that sense of humor returns in your connection, you know it is real because the energy of joy and lightness is very much a part of both your souls. It is an energy that has attracted you to each other many times."

Alexa's Between Lives Soul Regression

My discussion with Jeshua, Jorge, and Pamela had been enormously uplifting and helpful, providing much insight as to why Alexa, Jorge, and Luca had created such a challenging life blueprint. To learn more about what had been planned and why, Alexa and I did a Between Lives Soul Regression (BLSR).

I took Alexa through the usual physical and mental relaxation steps and then the past life portion of the BLSR. As she left her body in the death scene in the past life, I guided her to cross over to the other side.

"What are you experiencing?" I asked.

"I see silver light from stars," she began. "Below I see cloud circles—clouds as if they were an ocean. I feel like I'm standing on a cloud and lifting upward. I see a tree without leaves, a slender trunk with rainbow colors. I see hazy shapes of figures that look like angels—yellowy dresses and faces that are not defined. There are several of them. They are moving toward me and extending their hands.

"One has a very beautiful face, deep eyes, brown hair. It's a male figure who smiles at me and says, 'Don't be afraid. I'm one of your angels.' I feel that it is [Archangel] Gabriel."

"Tell Gabriel that we have questions we would like to ask about your life plan with Jorge and Luca," I prompted. "Ask him if he will take you to the Council of Elders so we can ask those questions. Then tell me what happens next."

"I see a stairway. Jorge is standing on the left side. Gabriel is on the right side, offering me his hand. The staircase opens up to a hole in the sky. I see the sky and stars. I'm using the staircase. Gabriel is floating next to me, and Jorge is at the top of the staircase."

"What's it like to see Jorge again?" I asked.

"*He is beautiful!* He's light and smiling with patience and understanding in his eyes."

"Ask Jorge and Gabriel to escort you to the Council of Elders. Describe in detail everything you see and experience."

"I'm now standing in the middle [of a room]. Beautiful, white faces looking at me, surrounded by shades of blue. The floor is like marble. There's a fireplace. It's like an amphitheater. The sides are stepped. The being I'm closest to is a beautiful woman with a lot of love in her eyes. She has a staff with a star in one hand and a golden ball in the other. Where I'm standing and up to the places where they are seated are red, white, and orange, and from then on it is purple and bluish, and everything is surrounded by stars."

"How many Council members are there?"

"Six. One behind me, two to my left, a lady in front of me, and another two on my right side."

"The female you described; ask if she is the spokesperson for the Council."

"Yes."

"What is her name"?

"Andromeda. I receive a very loving female energy from her."

Alexa and I then began to alternate speaking: I prompted her to ask certain questions of Andromeda, and Alexa repeated to me the responses she heard in her mind.

Alexa: What message does the Council have for me?

Andromeda: Be light. Be clear. You are brave to be here. Honor yourself. You are welcome here.

[I understood the first part of Andromeda's response to be a reminder to Alexa of who she really is: clear light. Every human is literally made of divine light compressed into a physical body. Here, the Council was asking Alexa to recall her true nature and shine.]

Alexa: What is my plan for my current lifetime?

Andromeda: To be yourself, speak up, help, serve, be happy, and get a deeper, extended knowledge of the relationships that form the world, cross the continents, and weave mankind together.

Alexa: Did Jorge, Luca, and I plan before any of us were born for Jorge to return when he did, shortly after Luca's birth?

Andromeda: Yes, you did, because his place is where he is now. That is his place from where to watch over you and Luca.

Alexa: Why did we create this plan?

Andromeda: To get further; to have a deeper experience in this lifetime; to have Luca connected to the light.

"I see Luca's head and a shining ball of light right above his head," Alexa told me as she described the image the Council was showing her. "It's the opportunity for him to connect to a higher light in this life."

I asked Alexa what questions she would like to ask the Council.

Alexa: I would like to know why, again, why we planned this.

"I see a forest," Alexa said as the Council placed a new image in her mind. "I feel that taking Luca into nature and making him sensitive to everything that surrounds us—the water, the air, the whispering of the trees, the clouds where his father looks down on him—reaches through to him like light and makes him cherish the Presence that is always here.

"Now I'm sitting on a big rock next to a river, combing my hair, seeing myself reflected in the river that runs through time and washes away my tears. It's serene, silvery, and beautiful. It's the River of Time. Jorge is there next to us, dressed like a knight. He emanates a gold and reddish fiery energy, very protective and male. He's like a sun, and I'm like a river, slowly flowing. Luca is like a little elf, hopping around in the bright forest. That is what it was meant to be like: three different energies that coexist on different planes."

Alexa: In what other ways is Jorge with me and Luca?

Andromeda: Jorge speaks to Luca through books and stories. He speaks through sending other male presences to support Luca's male energy. He's waiting in adventures. He will always be there to protect Luca.

Knowing that the Council will often bring in a loved one who has returned to the other side, I suggested Alexa ask the Council if she could speak directly with Jorge. No sooner had she asked than Jorge appeared. I continued to prompt Alexa to ask certain questions.

Alexa: [sadly]   Why was it so urgent to go so soon? What was your calling?

Jorge: It was not fast at all. I waited to be a father for a long time. When I was able to be a father, it was time for me to move on.

Alexa: How have you helped me to raise Luca?

Jorge: Your house. I had that house built for you. I provided this place. I filled the space with energy for you to live there. I watch over Luca at night. That's why Luca has such a sound sleep and has never been afraid of darkness. I guide his steps. I protect him.

Alexa: Jorge, what would you like other people who have lost their partner and who feel like they're raising children alone to know?

Jorge: [crying] That they are not alone at all, because they [their partners] are always there. They are always watching over them with such a profound love that never goes away, and they truly protect the children.

Alexa: How can those people sense the presence of their partner and know that they are playing a role in raising the child?

Jorge: [Light] a candle at night. Sit, relax, and listen inside to what their partner is telling them. Maybe put some objects of the 'deceased' on a cloth—a little altar in front of them. Just feel. Just let go. Many, many, many things are messages from loved ones who left that lane.

Alexa: What else can you say to people who are still grieving the loss of their partner to help them understand or to comfort them?

Jorge: Believe in the plan. And feeling the connection with something bigger, something on another plane, helps a lot to move on from feeling like a victim, feeling so left alone, feeling like the heart was torn out. The heart stays. That's very important. Concentrate on being complete.

Alexa: What can the parent who is still in body say to help the child understand what has happened?

Jorge: Tell the child to believe in the connection and look for it in your dreams. Feel safe, because you are always watched over. At night kiss the child's forehead and say, 'Your father or mother is with you and will take you on a beautiful journey.'

Alexa: [crying] Why can't I hear you more clearly? I feel like just by sitting down and wanting to talk to you, I should be able to, but I'm not. It feels like failure.

Jorge: I have the patience to wait for you and to accompany you further in this practice, because time doesn't matter for me. There is a lot of time ahead for us.

Alexa: Jorge, do you love me?

Jorge: *Dearly.*

Alexa: Are you happy with the way I'm raising Luca?

Jorge: Luca is a frolicking little boy, shining, golden. If that's the way we both see Luca, then you shouldn't doubt, you shouldn't ask, because we both see God [in Luca] through the same loving eyes of parents. Luca is very, very well.

Throughout the conversation Jorge's great love for Alexa and Luca had been palpable. Sensing that he had said all that was in his heart, I asked Alexa to return her focus to Andromeda and the Council.

Alexa: Where am I in my cycle of lives? Am I using everything I have learned in past lives, or is there [more] knowledge or wisdom I should be using?

Andromeda: You have come a long way. You have been here many times in front of us. You should feel certain of this task and your ability to live through it with wisdom and light, without falling, without becoming overwhelmed by this experience that is laden with grief. The grief is really a luminous ball of wisdom.

With that, Andromeda stepped forward and handed to Alexa the ball of light she had been holding. Alexa began to cry again.

Andromeda: This is your present: golden wisdom from the Council.

Alexa: What is in the future for me? Is there a man?

Andromeda: Jorge himself is opening the way. You can choose from different options.

Alexa: Thank you for all the gifts I was given. A lot of light. A lot of beauty.

"Alexa," I said, "before we close I'd like you to ask Andromeda and the Council to provide you with an energetic healing that will work at all levels: physical, emotional, mental, and spiritual. I want you to set an intention to receive the healing energy fully at all levels. Describe to me what you see and feel."

"I feel myself in the middle of the circle. I feel these beings stretching out their hands toward me. I feel golden light, a halo around my head. I feel myself wrapped in many layers of light—yellow light filling my body, inside my body orange, red light reaching my skin. The first level around me I feel blue, purple, and green. I feel a very special yellow energy in my breast and filling my whole torso. All around that is a white layer, like a robe, covering the colored layers. I see the Council's white long bodies sending and charging me with light. I see the other beings standing around with love in their eyes and smiles on their lips: my grandmother, angels, and Jorge. I'm still receiving this beautiful, loving energy that lights me from inside and fills me with beautiful colors and joy for life. These layers of light and color are to be spread once I get back down on Earth.

"They put a star on my forehead that will guide me through life and never leave me, never turn off its light. It will give me clarity. It will guide me through difficult times and illuminate beautiful times.

"Now the Council members lower their arms and ask me to draw my white robe around myself. I lower my head in respect and close my hands in front of my heart. I thank them dearly, profoundly, for being there for me at this special moment of my life. Thank you."

"Alexa," I said, "as we begin now to leave the high realm of your soul mind and the beautiful existence in the spirit world between your lives on Earth, I want you to remember that this loving world is always with you. Everything we have talked about—all your thoughts, your memories, and your insights— you will retain, and these will help and empower you as you complete the remainder of your current life with renewed energy and purpose.

"And as you hear me count forward from one to ten, your body and mind will come to wakeful consciousness, feeling as if you have just awakened from a very restful sleep. Alert and wakeful. The healing, understanding, and good work you have accomplished today will remain etched in your superconscious mind and will be reflected in your choices, actions, and self-concept from this day forward. You will open your eyes in complete wakefulness when you hear me speak the number ten. And you will remember everything as your eternal knowing merges more completely with conscious memories." I then counted slowly from one to ten, after which I paused to give Alexa time to orient and ground herself.

"What was that like for you?" I asked when I sensed she was back.

"Quite amazing! Quite profound!" she exclaimed. "Very beautiful. It was so out of time and space. When I recognized that I had been there before, my rational mind stepped aside and admitted that it was truly happening on a spiritual level. It was so real, and so forgotten, and yet so well known at the same time."

"What was it like to talk with Jorge?"

"Very clear messages that surprised me and that definitely are not part of my normal awareness."

"How do you feel?"

"I feel recharged and reaffirmed. I will definitely be a lot stronger feeling that love in my heart and the star on my forehead. I will be walking quite steadily. This is so much more than losing a husband, throwing the ashes into the ocean, and going on with life. I know there is so much more to learn, and I want to learn in a conscious manner."

ᕘ

Consider the sheer enormity and ineffable majesty of, as well as the extraordinary courage inherent in, Alexa's, Jorge's, and Luca's life plans.

These three eternal, infinite beings compress a portion of their energy into physical bodies. They relinquish instantaneous telepathic communication for the relative slowness of the spoken word. They leave a realm of no time to progress in linear time. They exchange eternal spirit bodies for mortal, physical forms. They give up the Divine Love they felt in the union of Home for the perceived separation of Earth. As if these challenges are not enough, they add to this mix the life plan of interdimensional parenting. Only the strongest of beings would dare undertake such an endeavor. Only the most courageous of souls would here tread.

It is through this awareness we understand that Alexa, Jorge, and Luca are not victims, for what could victimize souls so powerful? This understanding is one key to the fulfillment of their life plans. Jeshua so advised when he said, "It is important for Alexa to recognize his [Luca's] soul's greatness and not see him as a victim of a terrible fate." Jorge echoes this insight when he speaks to Alexa: "Please do not see Luca as a victim. He is strong and powerful and able to become the radiant star he is inside, despite losing his father so young." For Alexa to see Luca as a victim would be to deny his majesty as a soul and to energetically disempower him. By contrast, as Alexa comes to see Luca's inner light she energetically calls both of them into remembrance of their innate magnificence.

Equally beautiful as these three souls is the act of interdimensional parenting itself. Ostensibly, Luca is bereft of his father. Yet as Jorge told us, the energetic chord between the nonphysical parent and the child remains intact. Jorge senses when Luca is sad or afraid and needs him; he is then instantaneously by Luca's side. On the physical plane, little is as it seems. Every child who has "lost" a parent, every person who has "lost" a partner, and indeed every person who has ever walked the face of the planet is loved and supported from the other side beyond measure and far beyond our current understanding.

Alexa wisely knows, and as he grows Luca will come to know that Jorge is more than just by their side when needed. She tells Luca, "Look at the bird, the light in the tree, [or hear] the wind. Your father is there." Her words are far more than mere comforting sentiment; they are literally true. There is only one being in the Universe and no separation between any of the myriad forms that one being assumes. Jorge can be found in every breeze, raindrop, and grain of sand. The wave never separates from the ocean; the sunbeam never separates from the sun.

In full awareness of this truth, Jorge tells us that "many, many, many things are messages from loved ones." The special feather or leaf that "just happens" to blow across one's path; the cloud "coincidentally" shaped as a heart; the particular bird or other animal that appears when you think of a "deceased" loved one . . . all are the One Being impressing its consciousness on another portion of its consciousness.

And just as our loved ones create external communication with us in many ways, so, too, do they speak with us internally in more than one way. As Jeshua said, "To connect with the deceased, you must become familiar with a different kind of communication: through images, feelings, sudden realizations." There may also be images with words or words without images. The feelings sent by the loved one on the other side can sweep over the incarnate partner in either subtle or powerful ways, yet in both there is a knowing that the source of the feeling is other than oneself. Sudden realizations are downloads of information, knowing without knowing how one knows. The willingness to accept the knowing without grasping for intellectual comprehension is an act of trust, and trust is a purveyor of light. Light, in turn, contains information, including the treasured guidance offered by the partner in spirit about how to raise the beloved children.

Jeshua spoke to this truth when he said that insights come through being "unknowing." Fixed beliefs and rigid thought structures are like static between the dimensions, constricting or even at times cutting off the flow of wisdom to the partner who remained in body. Self-awareness is required to recognize such beliefs or thought structures; courage is required to dismantle or release them. Such self-awareness and courage may be particularly helpful in interdimensional parenting. Our beliefs create our reality. As Jeshua said, "If you are convinced that you are unworthy, their [the transitioned partner's] love may not reach you entirely." Yet even then the nonphysical partner can reinforce "seeds of light"—hope, faith, and trust—already present in the partner still in body. For you who have lost your beloved and fear raising a child or children "alone," choose now to plant such seeds of light within yourself. Choose now to believe that you are a holy child of Source/God, worthy of all love and support because of what you are.

CHAPTER 4

∞∞

Being Single

A PPROXIMATELY TEN PERCENT OF THE world's
population never marries. Regardless of whether one
marries or enters into a long-term relationship, many will
still spend a large portion of their lives single and not in a committed relationship. Often, people conduct intensive searches for
a romantic partner, either without finding someone at all or at a
minimum not finding someone as easily or quickly as they would
prefer. Could it be, I wondered, that being single is an experience
planned before birth? If so, for what reasons do souls choose to
have this experience?

To answer these questions, I spoke with Cathy, who has been
single and not in a romantic relationship for the vast majority of
her life. In speaking with Spirit and after conducting a Between
Lives Soul Regression with Cathy, I learned she had planned
being single as a *secondary challenge*—an experience she foresaw
and chose prior to birth because it would engender *primary challenges*: saying no to negativity in romantic relationships and yes
to loving herself. Although Cathy may have felt at one time that
she had failed by not sustaining a long-term relationship, she had
in fact succeeded spectacularly in saying no with loving-kindness
to negativity and in giving herself an opportunity to open her
heart to herself.

Cathy

Sixty years old at the time of our conversation, Cathy described herself as a holistic practitioner [healer] in private practice and a network marketing professional. She was the owner of a healing arts center. She lives in a beautiful, wooded, semi-rural area—like "living in a summer camp," in Cathy's view. "There's a beautiful lake nearby. I spend part of just about every day at the lake. It fills my heart with peace and beauty."

"Cathy, out of your sixty years on Earth, how many of the adult years were in a romantic relationship?" I asked.

"Very few."

"In the years you were single, did you want to be in a relationship?"

"For quite a bit of that I did. I spent time looking for someone. In hindsight I think I was trying to fit into a conventional model of partnership rather than being aware of my own process and acknowledging my capabilities and who I was."

Cathy's first serious relationship was with Curt, a college sweetheart whom she married in her twenties. She was drawn to his charm and abilities to lead and think outside the box. Much of their relationship with each other and with friends revolved around drinking and drugs.

"We had way too much fun and craziness," Cathy remembered. "What I didn't see was the alcoholism. Eventually, I realized it wasn't a healthy relationship. The drug overlay and the fog of alcohol were too heavy. I was young. What did I know about building a relationship and personal growth? I think I saved my life by leaving that relationship. We grew very far apart in our hearts.

"Curt eventually remarried, and he and his wife had a son. I had a dream the night the baby was born. We weren't in contact at all, but I had a dream the baby came. And Curt came to me in the dream and said, 'My wife and baby almost died.' I found out later that was true. The baby was born with cystic fibrosis and also what they called 'mentally retarded.' He lived to be thirteen

and then died. Curt later died of alcoholism and a disease associ-
ated with being in industrial pollution.

"Throughout my adult life, Curt has come to me in dreams.
In fact, I had a dream of him a week ago. What I realize is that
he's not settled in the ethereal plane. He needs my forgiveness.
He's asking for my help and forgiveness to move through and get
to the next place he needs to be." As I would soon discover, Cathy
was exactly right about that.

After her marriage to Curt ended, Cathy returned home to
Ohio and began the next phase of her life. She no longer wanted
to rely on a partner who might turn out to be abusive or alco-
holic, so she devoted herself to building financial security. As an
account executive for a cable television company, she sold adver-
tising time and earned a substantial income. "I cultivated myself
as an empowered young woman," she recalled. "I was unflap-
pable and unstoppable, successful and attractive, a force to be
reckoned with."

During that time period, Cathy entered into a relationship
with Jim, the one man whom she feels in retrospect could have
been a good, long-term partner.

"He could have challenged me, added value to my life,
influenced me to grow and realize my potential, and also been
a support and someone I could have given back to very fully,"
Cathy observed. "I didn't partner with him [long-term] because I
wasn't mature. I didn't have the capability or the understanding
of how to make a relationship work, and I had some things I had
to work through in myself. So, I didn't stay with him. Sometimes
I wish I had, but I also know that I would have had a very different life. I might not have done the things that have been my
purpose here."

"So, in your twenties, thirties—this period before you got to
your purpose—during the years you were single, what was that
like?" I wondered.

"Well, I was having a great deal of fun," she laughed. "When
I left Curt, I learned that the safest thing was to get out. I didn't
learn how to develop a relationship or work through things. I

learned to take care of myself by getting out. So, I did that for a long time. When I turned forty was when things shifted in my life as far as relationships go."

Cathy decided that a "bloodthirsty career" was not what she wanted for the remainder of her life. She also became very ill with mononucleosis, which she saw as a nudge to move in a new direction. She asked the Universe what was next for her and was guided to leave her job and attend massage therapy school. After graduation she built a successful practice.

"That's when I did a lot of deep work," Cathy shared. "And that's when I felt, more than the previous twenty years, that I really wanted partnership because I wanted to share the richness I was achieving. But now the game was different because who I was looking for was different, and I really wasn't finding that person."

Although Cathy was not finding an incarnate partner of equal spiritual depth, the inner work she was doing brought her into remembrance of—and contact with—a partner from previous lives who is in the nonphysical realm.

"I became aware of a spiritual partnership I'd had. This is a being I think I've been with for five or six hundred years in lifetimes. I have clear memories of an indigenous lifetime together. I remember feeling like it was very hard for anyone human to measure up to what I knew of that relationship."

Communicating telepathically, he told Cathy that his name is Star Heart. When Cathy was in her late forties and early fifties, Star Heart came to her many times. She sensed that he was there to support her and help her "take heart."

"We were Native Americans [in a past life]," she recounted. "It was at the time the Europeans were encroaching. I was a healer connected with the herbal traditions. Star Heart and I had three children. We were separated [by the Europeans], and our children were killed. In my role in this current lifetime as a healer, mystic, shaman, and connector of the community, Star Heart has been a support during all that time."

I asked Cathy to share a story of a time in her current incarnation in which Star Heart supported her.

"I was at a park, a beautiful part of the river that runs through the forest, hundreds and hundreds of acres, very secluded. A contemplative day. I was doing ceremony. The sky was a crystal-clear blue. There wasn't a cloud anywhere. I was praying with the water and the earth and the elements and my eagle feather. Star Heart, I felt, was present. When I looked up in the sky, there was one, huge, vertical cloud shaped *exactly* like a feather! It was very clear that he was showing himself to me and being part of the ceremony, supporting me in my prayers and my work."

There is only one being in the universe, and each of us is a part of the one. I understood Cathy's story to be a beautiful example of an individualized expression of the one (Star Heart) impressing his consciousness upon another individualized expression of the one (the cloud). In this way our loved ones on "the other side" will send a certain symbol our way to let us know they are here, ever present in our lives, always loving us. Bodies perish, but the bonds of love are eternal and inseparable.

Cathy had told me previously that even though she'd been in a relationship for a few years in her current lifetime, it feels as though she's always been single. I asked her why it feels that way.

"The first year or two of a relationship is la la la la," she answered with a laugh. "It's the honeymoon, the fun stuff. It's not the deep stuff. So, in terms of being a partnered person . . . I've really never been a partnered person."

"So, in all the years you've been single, has there been a yearning for the deep stuff?"

"Yes," she acknowledged. "The thing that I miss the most, that my life is lacking, is when there's a conflict in a marriage you have to hunker down, do some relationship work, and build your muscle and skill there. When there's a conflict in a friendship, you can go home and then have a conversation later. It's not as deep because you don't have to be with that person every day. I miss that. I never had it with my family of origin, and I've had few circumstances in my life where friends and I have gotten to work through conflict and challenge."

When Cathy was in her mid-forties, she married again. The marriage to Michael lasted a few years. She found that Michael added joy, helpfulness, and playfulness to her life but that he was irresponsible. "He was a good-hearted guy who just didn't know how to bring himself in the world."

For several years in her fifties she made a concerted effort to find a partner. She was active on several internet dating sites and had many dates, but a partner never emerged. I asked what motivated her and what the experience was like.

"I felt like, 'All right, if there's a partner for me then I'm gonna find him.' I'd heard about a woman who went on 108 dates before she found her partner. Then I met people who found the love of their life through internet dating, so I thought, 'Let me give this a try.' I dated people who looked on the surface like they would be the right person, like chaplains and people who had a spiritual path. After a number of years, I said, 'OK, I'm forcing an envelope that isn't mine to force,' and I accepted that this lifetime is for other things. Maybe there's an era down the road where that'll happen. I never close the door completely on things."

"How do you feel now about being single?" I asked.

"In truth, Rob, since I quit the dating scene I have acceptance in my heart. I'm at total peace and comfort with it."

"Are there moments when some difficulty arises and you think, 'Gee, I wish I had a partner to talk to about this'?"

"Yes, but I don't indulge in that feeling very long because it doesn't support me. That goes back to my spiritual training and the discipline of equanimity. I know that if I'm happy, it's up to me."

"Many people worry they will grow old or die alone. Do you have any fears like that?"

"I probably will grow old alone. I probably will die alone. I don't have any fears, Rob. I just don't. There's no room in my life for fear. What good is fear going to do? It's the opposite of love. It means I don't trust the Divine. I do the best I can every day to keep myself vibrant so that as I age I'm in the best position I can be.

"When we look outside ourselves for an answer or for some-body else to solve the problems for us, that's not where our strength lies," Cathy added. "Happiness, comfort, and peace don't come from there. It's gotta come from inside. My life's mission is to find that."

I asked Cathy what else she would like to say about being single.

"I feel very blessed to have my spiritual path. The Divine is within. What more could you want? I carry that in my heart all the time, every single day."

Cathy's Session with Aaron and The Divine Mother

I had eagerly awaited Cathy's session with Aaron, an enlight-ened being of immense love and wisdom channeled by Barbara. Aaron is able to access The Akashic Records, the complete, non-physical record of every thought, word, and action relevant to the Earth plane, including pre-birth planning. What I had not anticipated is that we would be treated to an audience with an expression of The Divine Mother as well. As Barbara explained to me, The Divine Mother is a blending of the highest feminine consciousnesses (Mother Mary, Quan Yin, and others) in our universe. Our session was conducted by video conference.

"I have a telephone in the middle of my face!" Aaron announced with a laugh as Barbara began to channel him and he became aware of his surroundings. I reminded myself that in the nonphys-ical realm in which Aaron lives all communication is telepathic. To Aaron a phone is an odd and foreign instrument. "I'm happy to meet you, Cathy. I have Rob's questions [in writing] in front of me. Cathy, simply look at me for a minute so our energy fields can connect better." Aaron was silent as he studied Cathy's image on Barbara's computer screen. He was looking at Cathy's physical body and the etheric bodies that surround it, noting the colors in her aura as well as any energetic blockages that might be present.

"Cathy, the birth plan is like the architecture for a house. You have an idea for a beautiful mansion; however, the side

rooms—the library, the crafts room, and the splendid solar-
ium—are not primary. What is primary is that central house
that will support your life. The central house for you, Cathy, and
perhaps for many people who end up not feeling they have what
they thought they wanted in their lives, is a soul plan to open
your heart more deeply to yourself. In several past lifetimes, the
one that you were was dependent on praise and honor from others. No matter how much of that was given to you, it never could
be enough. There was a feeling when somebody praised you of *'I
don't really deserve that.'* This was a subtle strand of self-negation.

"In one of these lifetimes, Cathy, there was a romantic relationship in which you were a man. You and your wife had a
number of children. Because so much of her attention was given
to the care of the children, you felt unloved. When I say 'you,' I
mean that past karmic ancestor.

"The children loved you. The wife loved you. But you began
to take one mistress after another, not really loving, but hoping
somehow to get the love you sought, which you could not accept
from your wife and children. You were not abusive to the wife
and children, excepting the extramarital affairs. You spoke to
them lovingly. You spent time with your children. Your children
adored you, but it wasn't enough because you could not fully love
yourself.

"In a second past lifetime you were—let's just call him in
today's terms—a politician. He was the head of a small nation,
but he wanted more. He wanted more territory, more people to
worship him, more people to be under his control because he
needed something to build him up. He never resolved it in that
lifetime.

"These are just two of numerous lifetimes in which the one
you were was not able to really open with love to yourself. Let's
go back one more step, Cathy. In one very early lifetime before
these, you were a girl. Your parents were verbally abusive. Your
father was physically abusive. You came into that lifetime not
specifically choosing to be abused but choosing to learn how to
say no to abuse. But, because you were unable to say no, much

anger came up and you blamed yourself. It was impossible to say *'it's his fault; he should not have raped me'* because the child you were needed to be loved, and the only way you knew to be loved was to be submissive. When you were submissive you felt they loved you, or at least they didn't attack you. So, you turned the anger on yourself.

"For many people who cannot find a long-term relationship," Aaron explained, "there is an issue of self-negation. The self-negation springs at least in part from some past lifetime of abuse in which they turned the anger they could not hold, onto themselves." (By *hold* Aaron meant *be present with.*) "So, the anger became a festering thorn in the heart. They did not permit themselves to be angry at the other because it was too dangerous. If we look for some of the causes of the present-day inability to fully love the self and accept the self's emotions without self-criticism, we often find abuse in some lifetime of the past—not always, but often. So, one comes into a lifetime knowing that this is the core of the structure, the house. The intention is to learn how to love and accept oneself, which means to accept one's sadness, one's fear, one's anger—whatever comes up—without looking at those emotions with a *'No, I shouldn't feel that.'*

"Because this was the highest intention in this [current] lifetime, Cathy, there was a desire for love, a desire for a deep intimacy. But because it was so hard to fully accept, to truly love the self, it was hard to accept love from others and therefore you could not invite that loving energy, that loving partner. The loving partner could have been there. I don't want you to blame yourself and say, *'I caused it.'* It's just the flow of karma, Cathy, but the healing of the karma is why you are here. It's not too late for you to find a deep, intimate relationship, but the first step is to learn how to be truly present with yourself, to love yourself, and to understand what blocks—habitually—you from loving yourself.

"I will go on to the next question," Aaron continued. "If you had chosen to marry Jim, what would have happened? I think you would have become estranged from him because he would have loved you and you would have felt undeserving of the love.

At a certain point there could have been conflict between you because you could not accept that he had a deep desire to give, to cherish, and for you it was not safe to allow yourself to feel cherished. If you could have learned how to do that at that point, then probably the relationship would have thrived; but where you were then, a relationship would not have thrived."

Aaron then addressed my question about Star Heart, Cathy's soulmate.

"What is a soulmate?" he asked. "A soulmate is literally that essence of consciousness that you are, taking birth together [from Source] like identical twins coming out of the womb they've shared for nine months. You and your soulmate burst into consciousness together with the intention eternally to support each other: sometimes taking birth together, sometimes not. There is not necessarily only one soul mate. There can be several.

"Simply, Star Heart loves you, Cathy, and wants to help you support your soul's intention. Star Heart is here to help you accept what you are feeling. When you are with Star Heart, you feel loved. Can you let yourself feel that love?

"Cathy, there is an entity Barbara incorporates [embodies] that we call The Mother. The Mother is literally a high expression of The Divine Mother and all her different aspects. She comes forth in the aspect that is most suitable to the person with whom we are speaking. For a few minutes now, The Mother is here with me. She says she would like to incorporate and just spend a few minutes looking in your eyes. I would like you to note what happens. You'll feel the love coming from her, I'm sure. But I think you may also feel some resistance. If you do, I would like you to breathe and just hold space. Ask yourself, '*What would it mean to fully accept this love, to know there's no question of my worthiness or unworthiness? This love belongs to me. It comes to me just because I am.*' See if you can just let yourself feel it. If you can't, that's OK. Watch what happens in the body. Do you push it away? Is there any feeling of resistance?"

Having previously experienced *darshan* with The Divine Mother, I knew what was going to happen. When I met The

Divine Mother, she said very little but simply gazed at me through Barbara's eyes with an intensity of love and adoration unlike anything I had ever experienced in my current lifetime. This pure, all-encompassing love flowed to me and around me, enveloping and embracing me.

We were silent for a few moments as Aaron's consciousness stepped aside and The Divine Mother began to utilize Barbara's body.

"My dear one, I love you," The Divine Mother began, speaking softly to Cathy. "I love you unconditionally." She was now gazing at Cathy with the same intense, genuine adoration I had experienced with her. "I can't hold your hands [in a video conference], but I extend my arms to you and Rob. You are a spark of God. You are radiant. As with all humans, there have been distortions, which is where one or another aspect of yourself has done some harm, but you are radiant and beautiful. If you work in your garden and dirty your hands, do you chop them off? You rinse them. You know that perfect, clean hands are there underneath. Why do you chop off the love for yourself? Why is it hard to know how radiant you are and how much you are loved—eternally loved? I think it is so hard for you to allow yourself to be fully loved and to love yourself, Cathy, because you are afraid of what will be expected of you if you are loved that much."

"This lifetime I've worked on love, radiance, understanding myself as the divine radiant light," Cathy replied, "and hearing this makes me feel like I've been lying to myself or living a sham." With this, Cathy began to cough forcefully.

"Not at all, Cathy," The Divine Mother reassured her. "You have done some very deep work, but always there are layers and layers and layers. The deepest layers usually are so painful that it's hard to get to them. There are two lifetimes [I want to discuss], Cathy. One is the lifetime Aaron spoke of in which the girl was abused. Part of the coughing is a memory that's been deeply suppressed. The child screaming as the father hovered over her to rape her; the father putting his hand over her mouth, even choking her, so that she could not scream. This happened not just once, but numerous times. He would come into your bedroom at night. He would find you in the barn behind the house. There was no escaping. You were just barely adolescent. He would pin you down. You would start to scream. He would choke you sometimes almost to unconsciousness to stifle the screams. This is part of the coughing—opening the throat and coughing out the anger. Some of the deepest anger for each human has been so buried.

"The other lifetime is one with anger at yourself. You were a woman carrying your three young children in a boat across the river. Let's call it a ferryboat. There were two dozen other people on board. The current was heavy that day. The riverman lost control of the boat. It hit rocks. You and many of the people tumbled into the vast, rushing water. You were holding your baby in one arm and trying to hold the arms of your other two children and keep yourself afloat. There was nobody to help you. There was much anger at the boatman. You saw that he was young, inexperienced, and careless. There was a heavy cable across the boat. The cable ran to a pulley. His work was to keep the boat moving on the cable straight ahead, but as it swerved it put too much pressure on the cable, so the cable finally tore.

"So, there you are in the river, drowning. You already had to let go of your two other children, trying to hold the baby up above the water with one hand, trying to keep your head above. But your head kept going under . . . water in your throat . . . anger, fear. Finally, the only thing [you could do] was save yourself. You let go of the baby. It was not a conscious act. You were drowning, and if you drown, of course, the baby would drown.

"Then somebody pulled you out, but the children were gone. You could not forgive yourself that you had not been able to save your children. Actually, one, the oldest, made it to the shore, but you could not forgive yourself. There was so much deep rage at this lad who was the riverman—and rage at yourself. The rest of your life was a torment.

"Aaron is asking to come in and speak," The Divine Mother informed us. With that, she stepped aside, and Aaron began once again to speak through Barbara.

"The work here, Cathy," Aaron advised, "is to use this as a metaphor for all the times this stream of consciousness that you are has been unable to overcome the harm that was done to you. Where does forgiveness start? Each human being has encountered situations like this. How do we forgive ourselves? Until we can forgive ourselves literally for our humanness, we cannot fully love ourselves. This, Cathy, is the deepest healing. When you can fully love yourself in that way, you become able not only to accept the love of others but also to invite a deeply loving partner because you can accept that love.

"Cathy, do you understand what The Mother meant when she said you are not lying to yourself or living a sham? You are simply preparing to go deeper. For the human the deepest place is not what you have done to others through negative emotions or fears; rather, it's the harm we have all done to one another and finding compassion for the whole human experience, for all beings. This is what leads you into knowing the awakened soul that you really are. Then you live from that awakened place."

"I have a question," Cathy said. "Was Curt, my first husband, my abusive father in the past life?"

"Yes, he was." And you were able to say 'no more' appropriately this time. Give yourself much credit for that. Do you understand how much self-love it took to be able to say no?"

"Yes. And was Michael, my second husband, the boatman?"

"He was not, but he well could have been. So, why were you drawn to these two men? Because your intention in an incarnation is always at least partially the healing of past karma: in the case of Curt, by being able to say no this time; in the case of Michael, to not settle for a partner who was irresponsible and immature. [Your pre-birth intention] was to say, 'I choose more than this. I do not choose to limit myself, based in self-negation, in this life.' You might ask why you were drawn to him in the first place. You knew Michael in a past life in which he was irresponsible. You had a soul pact that if you came together in this [current] lifetime, he would help you to be able to say no, and you would help him by saying it, and then you would go on. There was not an intention to stay together unless each of you was able at that moment to really do the work you needed to do, but that was unlikely because the human needs time, even many lifetimes."

Aaron's description of Cathy's pre-birth plans with Curt and Michael reminded me that little on the Earth plane is as it seems. In her current-life relationships with these men, she had felt mistreated and disrespected. She had perhaps wished at times that each man had not entered her life. Yet, the pre-birth intention is always to grow in some way, and such an intention requires others to play the role of catalyst. Though difficult and at times painful, such catalysts are planned with great wisdom, love, and regard for the highest good of all.

"Cathy," Aaron continued, "I want you to notice how both chokings felt: the river water choking—literally drowning; and the father choking you, your lungs filling up with alien substance—the figurative drowning. Part of that alien substance is anger. Part of that coughing was all the anger you have swallowed through many lifetimes wanting out.

"The next step is not to yell and unleash your anger in a cruel way. It's simply to acknowledge, breathing in, '*I have felt intense rage*' and breathing out, '*I hold space for the rage.*' The rage has arisen from conditions. 'I do not judge myself for it. I no longer need to hold it in me. I let it out. I breathe it out.'"

Here, Aaron was referring to the fact that thoughts and emotions are caused by external circumstances. When the conditions pass, so, too, do the thoughts and emotions. This simple but profound awareness allows us to dis-identify from our thoughts and emotions. That is, we no longer believe we *are* our thoughts and emotions; rather, thoughts and emotions are things we have, things we carry. If we but wait, they pass through us without always needing to be expressed or acted upon.

"Cathy, if you don't know what to do with it, just say, 'Mother, Aaron, please take some of this anger from me. It's tormenting. I release it to you.' Your friend, Star Heart, will help you. Star Heart is not only your soulmate but also is your primary guide in this lifetime. So, ask Star Heart. Ask any loving entity."

"Aaron," I jumped in, "many who read this chapter will be people who are single, unhappy, and perhaps even in despair. They may not understand why they can't find a partner. They may see the experience of being single as meaningless suffering. They may fear growing old and dying alone. What would you say to help them see the deeper spiritual meaning and purpose of their experience?"

"My dear ones, you are loved. You are always loved. Many of you feel unworthy of that love. Interestingly, most people who remain single are very old souls who are perfectionists about themselves. They have such high expectations of themselves not to have negative emotions, not to express negative emotions. When a negative emotion arises out of various conditions, they blame themselves. That self-blame creates an armoring around themselves. It holds others somewhat at a distance. There is such deep pain that they cannot attain the perfect state of constant lovingkindness and compassion to all beings, so they condemn themselves. Then, instead of forming a connection with another deeply loving being, they form a connection with someone who brings up the anger because there is the intention [at the soul level] to find compassion for themselves. So, they keep inviting that [type of person], rather than saying, *'I'm done with this. I am love. I am loving, and yes, I am human. If I step on a tack, my foot will be punctured, and I will feel pain. If I'm attacked by somebody, anger may arise. It's OK that it arose. It's very natural, just as the pain in the foot is natural. This is part of being human. The question is not whether it arose, but can I use this arising of pain as a catalyst for compassion [toward self] rather than further self-judgment.'*

"As this old soul begins to find more compassion for the negative thoughts that arise in any human and stops condemning themselves for that arising, then they begin to invite a similarly progressed old soul with whom they can do the work. They no longer need a catalyst for the anger and the ensuing self-judgment. They release it. So, I would say to all of you who are struggling, to ask yourself, *'In what ways am I not yet fully open to love, to a truly loving and supportive heart?'* Trust that you are an old soul moving through a certain phase of your growth.

"Some of you," Aaron continued, "have found compassion for yourself, but you're still inviting people who have not, and then you don't want to deepen into a relationship with them. Why are you inviting that? Perhaps because at some level the heart still feels too tender. It's hard to imagine really coming into that deepest intimacy wherein the other will begin to see the still-arising negativity. *'What if this person sees that I still get angry, that I still am judgmental?'* There's fear that until you see it clearly and find compassion for it in yourself you cannot let another see it.

"But, my dear ones, you *can* do this, and this is why you came into the incarnation. I say to those of you who are alone and seeking intimacy, *you can do this.* You can learn to love yourself more fully so that you can invite a loving partner. You are not single because you are bad. You are single because you are not yet fully as loving of yourself as you intended to become in this incarnation. As you love yourself more fully, you will invite that loving relationship. Please do not take this as another reason to judge yourself: *'Oh, I've fallen short. I'm not loving enough.'* That's not what I'm saying. All of you are radiant, beautiful beings as the Mother has said to you, Cathy. You can love and accept love if you will take it one step after another, further into the risk of loving and of being loved. Trust the possibilities.

"If despite all this you end up alone, please trust that you do have a life plan. Ask yourself, *'What is wholesome about me?'* not *'What is not wholesome?' 'How can I build on this, not to make myself a better person so others will love me, but simply because building on the love in my heart is a joy.'* By removing the attachment to outcome, Aaron was making the building process a lighter, less constricted experience in which support from Spirit would flow and be received more easily.

"It's not all about [romantic] relationship, this human lifetime," he continued. "In what ways do you truly give joy to others? In what ways do you serve others? Some of you are teachers. Some of you care for others in the body and the emotions. Some of you are farmers who care for the land or plant orchards. Some of you weave fabrics, paint paintings, or create music. Cherish yourself for this. Your lifetime is not necessarily just about a relationship. I realize that you are lonely and want that, but the more you focus on your heart's joy and what you do give, and the more you credit yourself for that, the more you open yourself to the relationship you seek.

"I love you," concluded Aaron. "I walk with you. I have walked your path in many lifetimes, and I knew your pain. Know you're loved. Rob, I turn it to you. Does that adequately answer your last question?"

"Yes, but I have another," I replied. "What are other reasons people plan before birth to be single for much or all of their lives?"

"Sometimes it is not the healing of karma," Aaron answered. "Sometimes it's because there is a higher focus; for example, somebody who deeply commits to some pursuit—the arts, medicine, a religious path. There may be a deep aspiration to learn that you are sufficient and that you do not need a partner to be sufficient, that what you bring to the Earth—you as one radiant, single human being—truly blesses the Earth, just as one seed of an apple tree, picked up by a bird, carried to a fertile field a distance away and then dropped, grows and blossoms into a new apple tree. That tree drops its apples, and new seeds form. A hundred years later, there's not only an orchard there, but there are orchards a mile in all directions—all started from this one seed. Some people feel they cannot do that alone, but you can. You are the seed, each of you, and you may have chosen as your birth plan to literally be that one seed that starts the orchard in whatever direction your life is taking.

"You may say to me, 'But Aaron, I am not a physician or an artist. I am not a great person in any respect. I simply live my life quietly.' That is a seed. Perhaps it's to help the invalid across the street, or to take a walk and smile at little children and your neighbors and pat the dogs. You smile at the person walking down the street, and they smile at the next person they meet, and it spreads. Just to bring your loving energy is planting seeds.

So, the intention here is to begin to know, '*I am sufficient. I am that seed that can start an orchard—an orchard of kindness, of love.*' This is a primary reason why people plan before birth to be single—to learn that they are sufficient."

"Aaron," I said, "the human experience on Earth seems to be set up so that most of us want partners. Why is that? Are there other planets where it's not set up that way?"

"It's simply that you are mammals, Rob, a mammal drawn to another mammal for intimacy. But there are other planes of existence—I don't want to use the word *planets*—where people—let's not call them *people*—where individuated consciousness does not take a specific form. It can move into many different forms, merging with many beings. It's a different form of intimacy.

"Interestingly, beings who are thusly evolved may not yet be ready for the individuated form that takes so much courage. They're used to experiencing without separation." Aaron was referring to the fact that the limitations of the five human senses cause us to perceive ourselves as individuals who are separate from one another. In fact, we are one with one another and with all beings in existence. "What happens when you move into the illusion of separation? The work of the human is to experience the illusion of separation and through a deep awakening to move through it. The mammalian form in the human experience forces the illusion of separation so that one can crack open that illusion and, in a sense, come back to where you started, when you were on that plane of being with no illusion of separation, but now in a much more mature way, having experienced the illusion and broken free of it rather than never having experienced it."

What is the value of immersing ourselves in this illusion and then breaking free of it? The act of forgetting and then remembering that all are one leads to a more profound self-knowing. If we never experienced anything other than oneness, we would not fully understand or appreciate what oneness is. The experience of perceived separation, however illusory it may be, creates a contrast with oneness that eventually leads to a much deeper understanding of oneness. It also creates intense feelings such as anxiety and fear that cannot be readily experienced in a state of oneness. Much of the growth on the Earth plane comes through the experience of intense emotions and in particular of learning how to work skillfully with them.

"Aaron," I asked, "after we return to spirit at the end of a lifetime, what are our relationships like with the people who were our romantic partners when we were in body?"

"There is no norm, Rob," Aaron told us. "It depends. It's really a soul question. One can have a deep, very loving, romantic relationship with a being here [on Earth], and other than a brief greeting on the other side, really not be connected. That being may be off on a completely different plane. That being may greet you as you transition if that being has transitioned first, support you through the early stages of the transition, and then move on to wherever it—androgynous, not male or female—is working. Or it may be that they stay very close to you, and there may be deep intimacy that continues on the other side.

"There could be somebody like Curt. One aspect of Curt was the human who was abusive in various lifetimes and is working to transcend harm to others. But there's another aspect of Curt: the deep soul aspect capable of love and loving. There could be a very warm relationship with Curt on the other side, both laughter and tears over what occurred in this lifetime. Probably it would not be an ongoing friendship but a decision to continue to meet in future lifetimes if it is of service to you both. It could even be for Cathy a willingness to incarnate and be in a relationship or marriage with Curt in a future lifetime as the one who is now strongly capable of saying no to abuse, but in such a loving way that it helps Curt to overcome what is abusive in him, because that which is abusive in him is that which cannot love himself or others. I'm not suggesting that will or should happen. Simply, there could be that possibility. It's never forced on you—it would come willingly—that maybe your guides ask you, Cathy, to consider being part of his support team [by playing that role in another incarnation].

"Cathy, I'd like to suggest a book to you called *Testimony of Light* by Helen Greaves. Helen was a medium. Her friend said, 'If I die first, I'm going to come and tell you what it's like [on the other side], and she does. The book is very helpful to many people.

"So, it depends on if there was a deeper soul connection," Aaron concluded. "You'd be together if there was reason for that connection. But consider, in how many hundreds or even thousands of lifetimes, you have been with how many different souls? Who will you be with after the transition? It may be somebody who wasn't incarnate in this current lifetime—likely Star Heart would be somebody that is very close after your transition, Cathy, as I will be very connected with Barbara when she finally transitions.

"Cathy, trust that as the soul grows, there is invitation of the deeper relationship. It will happen, but the deeper relationship is not the primary thing you wanted. The growth of the soul is. And please do reflect on the cough. Ask yourself in a very gentle way, '*What was I coughing up? What wants to release itself from this body and consciousness?*'"

Cathy then asked Aaron if she had deeply loving relationships in past lifetimes.

"Every being has," he told her. "Cathy, picture yourself, if you will, simply emitting light. There is no solid structure. You're in a different plane of being. Picture a color to that light. Tell me, what color are you?"

"A bright, silver blue."

"Now, picture entering a space in which there are other light beings, each emitting their own spectrum of light. You're drawn to some colors—not necessarily the color you are—more than others. Across the room you see a beautiful silver rose color, and despite all the yellows and greens and lavenders, you are drawn to that silver rose. Your colors begin to dance with each other so that your color remains clear and vivid and its color remains clear and vivid, but in part they swirl together and even blend." Here Aaron was describing how in the nonphysical realm we retain our individuality while at the same time merging our energy with another's. "You do that dance for a while, and then something also very beautiful and more purple comes in and joins the dance, and then some pale lemon-yellow joins the dance. Soon the room is filled with merging light. Feel yourself letting go of any validity to 'I am this [particular energy]' and just become all of that light—merging with, feeling totally acknowledged, accepted, beloved, and part of all that swirl of light. And then gradually draw your own light back as others begin to draw theirs back. But the light you are is now enriched. It's not just that silver blue, but now there are little touches of pink and yellow and peach and lavender running throughout—not marring but enhancing.

"This was a plane of being you dwelt on for quite some time, Cathy, coming to trust the power of yourself, the radiance of yourself, and your ability to take in and give to others. Then you made the decision that it's time for another human incarnation. You had been human before. *'I will see if I can maintain that sense of who I am and the ability to cherish who I am, to share it; not to be afraid of others but to say no to others' darkness who would come at me with pain.'* So, you came back into human form for a number of lifetimes."

I then shared with Aaron my understanding that some planets have as many as five genders. "Is that true?" I asked him. "And if so, what do romantic relationships look like on a planet like that?"

"First of all, they are not necessarily monogamous," he explained. "There's no need for monogamy because one knows oneself is in everything and everything is in you. On an advanced-consciousness planet like that, there is no sense of a separate ego self that needs to be better or worse than, but simply a deep desire from each being to cherish and to be [cherished].

"Yes, there will be different genders. I can't begin to explain those other than to say that you have different genders today. You have the male. You have the female. You have male inclining toward the female. You have female inclining toward the male.

You have female and male that are very balanced. You have the male consciousness in the female body, the female consciousness in the male body. You have many genders, but because of the heaviness of the human emotional body [the subtle energetic body just outside the physical body], you have not yet, for the most part, learned to fully embrace all the other genders and to embrace that all of those genders are also in you—maybe not strong, not dominant, but all the genders are in you from one time to another.

"So, relationships on such a planet will be very connected. The ones coming together as two, sometimes as three, or five, or twenty, and not just physically, sexually, but also emotionally—all coming together, dancing, embracing, and sometimes mentally sharing thoughts, where there is no need to be right, no need to control, only fully open so that all the ideas flow out and new things can be created. How do you mingle [very different] ideas? You don't try to impose your idea on others. You come together, each totally seeing and absorbing all the others' thoughts until communally you just rest in your energy together. A new vision arises built on everything that has been input so far.

"These are very advanced civilizations, beings who are far beyond the separated ego. However, as Earth is gradually becoming a higher density climate, this is where the Earth is headed." Aaron was referring to the fact that Earth was for many millennia a third density (third dimensional) planet. It is now moving through fourth density (the fourth dimension) after which it will become a fifth density (fifth dimensional) planet. "This advance of ideas, this merging—holding powers of your own but fully merging with everything else to explode outward into something brand new and radiant—this is where Earth is headed as we transition to a higher consciousness.

"Rob," Aaron continued, "your book is about the pre-birth planning of different aspects of romantic relationships. Romantic relationship is often thought of as one human being becoming intimate with another. I'm not thinking specifically of a sexual relationship, but deep, emotional, and energetic intimacy. Although this is one form of intimacy the human usually takes or seeks, please remember there are many other ways to be intimate. If you feel you have not been able to establish the intimacy you seek in this lifetime, I would ask you to find a tree in your yard or in a local park and spend some time sitting by it. Hug it. Talk to it. Establish intimacy with that tree. Lie down on the grass, feel the earth underneath you, and allow intimacy with Earth. Find the earth element in yourself and know that you are the Earth and how beautiful that is. Then look up to the sky, and as you breathe know that you are the air element. If possible, float in a body of fresh water. Feel the water around you. Feel the water in your body and know your intimacy with the water element. Feel the fire of the sun and experience that within you. Know the intimacy of that. Finally, feel the energy in the whole world around you and in yourself. In this life gradually invite deeper intimacy with yourself and the elements that comprise you. Through intimacy with the external elements—letting go of 'internal' and 'external' and allowing that merging—this will bring you much joy.

"The next step, which may be months down the road when you can really rest into that intimacy with your body and the external elements, is to find a friend, not necessarily a lover or possible lover, just a friend who is willing to pursue the experiment with you. Ask that person to develop some intimacy for the elements in the same way. When you both have done that, sit together. Begin to feel the earth element not only in yourself but also in the other. Then feel the fire element in yourself *and* in the other, etc. Feel any way that you pull back from the fullest sharing. This exercise can lead to two things.

"First, it can lead you to see any ways you were holding yourself separate from others with whom there may be developed relationship. Second, it can bring you a deep sense of peace from the profound intimacy you already have but you have not been able to see because there was this *'I want that'* instead of focusing on what is already there and the deep joy of it. This may lead you into a more intimate human relationship—it also may not—but it will bring you immense joy to experience that intimacy.

"Do this with your pet. It's very easy to be intimate with a pet. Get your energy flowing between you and the pet. Feel the joy of that. You have an intimate relationship; it's simply not the human one. I know you wish for the human one, but reflect on and feel the joy of the intimacy that's already there. Build on that because it will open a doorway to allowing deeper human intimacy.

"I would also add," Aaron said, "that each of you has one or more guides who deeply love you and who are there to support you. Ask us for help. We want to support your growth on this plane, to support your manifestation of your soul's plan in this lifetime. Remember that you come with numerous plans, some more a priority than others. Trust your experience and allow yourself to move into those plans that are of the highest priority. It's very natural that a loving relationship is part of that. Ask yourself what blocks a loving relationship. If someone appeared now who seemed to be the perfect, loving partner for you, is there anything that might block it? For many of you the block may simply be what I call the *'What if someone finds out?'* place: the place deep within that you have not been willing or able to acknowledge in yourself, the place that sometimes feels hatred, fear, or greed. *'What if this person sees that I'm a mess? Can I carry on forever being seen as the beautiful person but whom I think of as a fraud? Maybe I better block this person, not let them get too close.'* We all have light and shadow. The other person, when they see the shadow within you, can help you to heal it just as you can help them to heal theirs. Do not be afraid of the shadow in yourself or allow it to block your relationship. Simply hold the intention that you will not do harm. Trust that the light in you is stronger than the shadow. Trust your ability to live in that light and to help your partner live in his or her light. You can do it. My blessings and love are with you."

After Cathy and I had expressed our deep gratitude to Barbara, Aaron, and The Divine Mother, I asked Cathy to stay on the phone with me.

"How are you?" I wondered.

"My God!" she exclaimed. "I got such a huge healing from them! And the fact that Curt was my abusive father before. I got that so clear when he said that. Curt had been banging on my door to forgive and release him.

"I really feel in my heart a lot of peace. I feel like something I've been holding onto for a long time [has been released]. I feel so light, Rob. I feel very, very different. I feel a river flowing in me in places it hasn't.

"He gave me a lot. You know, Rob, I have always had that in my throat. I'm coughing and clearing my throat—always, forever—and haven't known what it's about. But I feel clear now."

Cathy's Between Lives Soul Regression

Aaron and The Divine Mother had provided us with a great deal of insight into Cathy's soul's intentions in her current lifetime. To see what else we might learn, I conducted a BLSR with her. I began the session with my usual prayer:

"Dear Mother/Father God, Cathy's spirit guides, guiding angels, higher self, and what there is of love and light in the Universe. Thank you for joining us here today for Cathy's Between Lives Soul Regression. We ask that you please bless, guide, and facilitate our session. Please help us to receive the information, the healing, the understandings, the expansions of consciousness, and other outcomes that will be helpful to Cathy and the readers of her story. Thank you for blessing and guiding our session. Amen."

After taking Cathy through the physical and mental relaxation parts of the hypnotic induction, I guided her into a past life.

"I'm outside," she announced as she began to see the past life. "Countryside. Daytime. There are beings nearby. My lower legs are bare. I'm wearing a white fabric, like an ancient dress. There are no sleeves, and it isn't shaped. It's just a covering, a luminous kind of robe or dress. I'm female. I feel like I'm a spirit being, like it's before time, at the beginning of creation. It seems to be a depiction of my essence, an archetypal expression of myself. There's a lot of hair on my head. It's brown but also gold. There's an ethereal quality to me.

"I'm in a tree, and the sunlight is dappled through the leaves. It's like there's a force everywhere. It's a very vibrant feeling. I see bright, bright green and the grays of tree trunks, and the path below has an earthiness of greens and browns and moss and rocks in the forest.

"I'm floating down from the tree by the pure magnetism of my heart. I'm aware of lights appearing, like heart beams coming all around me. There are other beings here that don't have shapes or forms as much as they are luminous. I'm on the Earth, and it's so long ago that life as we know it isn't here yet.

"We're in a clearing in the forest, and the light of all of us is just beautiful. It's beautiful! It's bright, radiant, clear light, but also iridescent. My sense is there's nothing that needs to be done but just existing as pure love. It's just being as light."

"Cathy, I want you to trust that your soul and spirit guides are showing you this scene for a particular reason or reasons," I instructed. "What is important for you to know or understand about the scene you're being shown? Trust that you know the answer."

"The light that I am in my current lifetime began long ago—many, many evolutions—and has always been in me. My presence has been as one who holds and shares light, one who inspires and empowers others with the light. It's been this way since then. Also, there's a great, peaceful, exuberant joy permeating the scene. It's almost ecstatic but grounded, if that makes sense."

Cathy then told me that she felt complete with the scene. I prompted her to move forward to the next significant event or scene in that same past lifetime. Although the instructions are always to stay in the same past life, approximately fifteen percent of people move to another lifetime, and this is just what Cathy did. Spirit always shows the person whatever is for her and the highest good to see.

"Now I'm on a winged spirit horse," Cathy informed me. "We're riding on a rainbow like a roadway, looking down at the Earth. It's so beautiful: oceans filled with life, snow-covered mountains. We're in Asia. This ride is an overview; we're not landing. It's showing me that I've had a choice in where and when to come [to Earth].

"I'm coming down now in a cold country . . . North America . . . Canada. I'm on the land. I'm an indigenous woman wearing a doeskin dress and moccasin boots, coverings, and wraps. There's a village. We live in harmony with the Earth. There are children all around and elders."

"Can you tell if you have a partner?" I asked.

"I do. It's my Star Heart. He's mighty, respected, strong, beautiful. He flies over the Earth in his physical body, meaning he's fast and takes care. He's a person of few words."

"What is your relationship like?"

"There's a synergy. I'm the female healer using the herbs and medicine of the Earth, which we knew back then. He's a male counterpart to that, not in the sense of being a healer, but rather as one who knows. So, there are not words that pass between us. It's not like that. It's like how the foxes run together. There's a knowing."

"Allow the scene to unfold naturally," I prompted. "What are you shown next?"

"We have children. We have a baby that's in my arms. We have other little ones. Sometimes they go with him to learn. Sometimes they go with me. We're both very nurturing. We're people of the earth, but also people of light and being, so close to both without the overlay of sophistication that clouds modern life. We just have a flow and a rhythm like a golden waterfall flowing into a crystal lake—a purity of living. We teach all the children, just like everyone else does.

"I carried the light we saw in that previous life into this lifetime. I wear it on the surface as well as inside, deeply. There's a purity of existence here, not a savagery. It feels quite spiritual and earthy and harmonious all at once. There's a deep heart connection."

"Cathy, what is important for you to know or understand about the scene you're being shown?"

"That richness is inside me. It explains my idealism in my current lifetime, because I know what pure living is and have experienced it."

I guided Cathy to move forward to the next significant scene Spirit wanted to show her.

"I'm in the Middle Ages," she said as she began to see a third past lifetime. "It's dank and wet, cold and dreary. I don't like it here at all. I see buildings made of stone. I see peasants on the land in grubby attire, struggling. I see drunken, toothless, dirty people. People grab each other by the hair—it's that bad!—and throw each other around. The mentality has a brutality to it, people living like animals toward each other. There's a feeling of every man for himself. It feels hopeless."

"Allow the scene to unfold. What happens then?"

Cathy paused for a few moments to take in what Spirit was showing her. "I am stoned as a witch because the way I bring my light and healing into the world doesn't fit. The contrast of the other lifetime we just saw and the first one and then trying to live during this time as a light being, as a healer: it just didn't work. Women were so mistreated. I tried to come in and hold light for them and be an encouraging factor."

"Are you at the stoning scene now?" I asked.

"No, I don't want to go there. I know it happened, but I'm avoiding it."

"I want you to go there, but do not go into the body. Just float above the scene." Doing so would allow Cathy to experience something important without actually reliving the trauma. "Allow the stoning to occur. I'm going to count to three, and on the count of three that lifetime will come to an end. *One . . . two . . . and three!* We ask that all vows and promises tied to the past life we've just examined that no longer serve be released and nullified.

"You have just died and are moving away from the physical body. You have been through this experience many times before, and you feel no physical pain or discomfort. As you move away from the body, you will be able to continue to talk to me and answer my questions because you are now in touch with your inner, true self: your soul. Feel your mind expanding into the very highest levels of your being. As you float upward away from the body and as you look down at the body, you may perhaps feel some brief sadness or remorse at this moment, but your spirit has been through this experience before, and soon you will be able to return home. Where are you now in relation to the body?"

"As soon as you said that life was ended, I flew out," Cathy answered. "Some of your words made my heart open, free of the suffering and constriction of that time. So, I'm above. I'm back in spirit. My surroundings are just beautiful! Soft, golden white light. The feeling in my heart is just peace, full and rich. It's love."

"Cathy, do you see or sense any other beings there with you?"

"This part is the least visual of all. It's more an essence or a sensing, like when you walk into a room and you feel different people's energy. This is like that feeling, but remove all the physical. It's just being aware of each other. Wow, it's like a universe, only I'm the center just because that's what my perspective is. So, whatever direction I look, there are beings all around, like in a giant sphere."

"Cathy, you're now in a realm in which all communication is telepathic. I want you to send a telepathic message to these beings, thanking them for being here today and ask that whoever is for your highest good to speak with to step forward."

"A great light being of wisdom and truth [steps forward]," she told me. "It is a 'he,' if there is a thing like that. He reflects myself back to me, all that's good [in me]. He says:

Light Being: Do you see? Do you see what you've known in your heart all along, my child? In all your lifetimes you've had a consciousness about the

light you are. You have been carrying it inten-
tionally through each lifetime. You saw the one
of suffering to know something you've experienced in this [current] lifetime as well, but to
a lesser degree: that your spirit, your essence, is
the true you and is capable of so easily rising
above any earthly suffering. Now that we're here
and you're seeing it this way, never forget. Any
difficulty that comes—never forget! Well done
this lifetime. You've worked very hard, diligently
and consciously through layers of other lifetimes
that didn't quite get finished. It's why you have
so much peace in your heart now.

Cathy: Why was I shown the first lifetime, early in the
Earth's existence? How is that lifetime related to
being single in my current lifetime?

Light Being: We started there for the reminder of your essence:
your wisdom and light and the perfection you
felt and experienced. The memory of that has
never gone away. In this [current] lifetime, being
single has to do with resting in that perfection
rather than jumbling it with the chaos that can
come in relationship.

The purity you had in that lifetime also came
through in the indigenous one. That is your
deepest memory and is in your cells. It's part
of you. Not finding [a partner in your current
lifetime] does not mean you won't have it [the
purity]. It's how you've lived this life.

Cathy: Why was I shown the third lifetime in the
Middle Ages?

Light Being: To show you that the spirit is what endures and
that the difficulties are nothing compared to

the beauty, the magnificence, of the spirit. You were shown that lifetime to help you forgive and remember to forgive. You were shown that to give you the contrast and to remind you that every choice, every thought, every action can bring you the light life or the Dark Ages, and it does so in each moment.

You have wanted a special time or ceremony for forgiving Curt and setting him free. Now is the time to do that, while he's here, other beings are here holding space, and I'm here.

Curt is here! Though surprised and somewhat jolted by this announcement, I recognized and welcomed this opportunity for him to heal.

"Cathy," I prompted, "please go ahead and do that with Curt. Describe in detail what happens next."

"Curt is coming forth. He's [showing himself as] crippled and with the appearance, the dress, of a Middle Ages person, representing the mentality of him, of his spirit, the place he's been stuck, so how could our life together have progressed? I had a path to spread my wings. He was trying so hard to keep me in a cage like a bird, to imprison my spirit, and to break it. So, he seeks my forgiveness in order to feel that he can move on.

"Curt, I forgive you. I forgive you. Move on with your life. Find your wings; they're there. I see greatness in you! I always saw greatness in you even when the Earth life wasn't so great. It was there, and it still is. I give you my blessing. Touch lives in a good way to bring light and love forward—the light and love you've always had in you. Be free from what you perceive as your limitations and the shame and guilt you have borne. Let them go. Shed them like those Middle Ages clothes you're wearing right now.

"I see the gray, cloak-like garb falling away. I see Curt as he was as a younger man when I met him: tall and straight, with a shining crown of hair and in a healed body, putting his hands on his heart and bowing his head a little bit humbly to himself in recognition, in remembering. There are tears sliding down his face. He says, 'It's been so long being stuck in that place of brokenness and belief of myself as broken. I just needed the forgiveness and the touch of a fair maiden [said with a laugh] to set me free.'

"I ask him if in all those dreams that he came to me he was coming with intention to ask for forgiveness. He's remorseful. He says, 'I'm sorry for plaguing you when we were together [on Earth] as well as in the dreams.'

"I'm saying, *'It's forgiven! It's forgiven! It's forgiven, and I love you!* I love you, and I thank you for being part of my journey and growth. As a young person, when we first were together, you gave me a piece of my freedom and a rite of passage into adulthood.'"

I felt deeply moved by the power, beauty, and grace of Cathy's words. Although she had been badly hurt by Curt's behavior, she had arrived at a place of genuine forgiveness and gratitude for the wisdom that had come from the experience. As she concluded her conversation with Curt, I reminded myself that forgiveness and gratitude are the most powerful ways energetically to bless, release, and therefore be complete with an experience. Both she and Curt were now truly free to move on.

I asked Cathy to ask the Light Being what else is important for us to know about any of the three lifetimes she was shown.

Light Being: What happened between you and Curt has been an influence for many, many years of your adult life, holding you back from wanting to engage in a relationship. There were multiple factors for you having a single life. One of them was the harm that was done through that relationship to your spirit, your faith, and your optimism.

Another was feeling that you never found the resonance of that ideal relationship you saw in the indigenous life and the first life. You've been seeking that and not finding it in the physical realm.

In regard to the third life in the Middle Ages, ask yourself, 'What was my purpose there?' The answer will show itself.

Cathy: I chose to come with a gallant hope of helping girls and women during that time, and it was not received.

Light Being: Be appropriate in the choices you make. You must not think you can change the world when it's not your calling or within your power to do so.

In terms of being single [in your current lifetime], what do you see there?

Cathy: In some of my relationships in this lifetime, I engaged with a person who I felt would learn from me, or who I could help or save.

Light Being: Do you see now that you were wise to abandon the project because it's not your job in life to fix a man, to save him through relationship? You know what relationship can be at its highest level, so you abandoned it each time. It was wise of you.

Cathy: In the third lifetime, when I saw the futility of what I thought I could do, was it my choice to leave [die]?

Light Being: Yes. There was another lifetime in the Middle Ages when you came in as a girl, but your family saw who you were [as a soul] and so disguised you as a boy to allow you to be a leader, like a priest, a holy person, in the community because they wouldn't acknowledge a girl in that role. You were discovered and killed then, too. So, you didn't get the lesson the first time, and then you tried again.

You're very brave. You're not afraid, and you're still that way. You take risks because you recognize the transience of the body and the depth of spirit.

Sensing that we had completed our discussion of the three past lives, I asked Cathy to tell the Light Being we wanted to ask the Council of Elders questions about her current lifetime. I prompted Cathy to follow him to the Council.

"It's like we're walking among the clouds," she said as she arrived at the Council, "an ethereal place. The Council has been here all along. I'm seeing light beings, both genders. [A feeling of] ancientness and wisdom, light, truth, justice, beauty, enlightened consciousness is all around in these beings. Because I'm asking to see what they look like, they're showing me a shape of a kind of light. The sense of knowing they're here is stronger than the visual shape, but they're accommodating me by giving a bit of a form."

I then prompted Cathy to ask a series of specific questions of the Council.

Cathy: What is my plan for my current lifetime in regard to being single? Why did I create that plan?

Council: It would have been very difficult for you to be in a relationship that could keep up with all that you've gone through and done in this lifetime. The impracticality of partnering is real because of the limitations of humanness.

Also, your spiritual journey has been extremely deep and personal and was best served by you walking alone without the distraction or the doubt that may have been cast on your path by another person. You wanted that clarity. You wanted that focus. You wanted to not be deterred, doubted, or made insignificant by a judgment or the energetic emotions of another person. You wanted the clear path to do deep, broad healing work spanning many lifetimes. You wanted deep spiritual connection and discovery.

Cathy: Many people would say that their romantic relationships are a stimulus to growth. What is the difference between me and the many people who fulfill similar intentions at least in part through relationship?

Council: In other lifetimes—you were shown one today—you did your growth and healing through relationship. The difference in this lifetime was your request to focus without distraction and go inward. We point to the many years you've spent as a contemplative in modern life, arising every morning and sitting under the apple tree for hours in contemplation and discovery; the time you've spent in the garden digging in the Earth, learning her lessons and listening to her; the time you've spent at the fire and under the moonlight in the forest with circles of women, living in community; the many hours in a sweat lodge, praying; your travels to India, seeking the divinity within you.

Cathy: Why did I plan to do my growth and healing through relationship in some lifetimes but not others?

Council: That is simply where you are on your evolutionary journey.

Your ego self, your human self, your human heart has at times, earlier especially, felt lonely and wanted a partner, but as you ripened, you no longer felt lonely. Also, you saw the bigger plan more and more as time went on.

The healing lifetimes, like the first lifetime [you were shown] where there was such a high consciousness, were to allow that to come into the human plane. But along the way the humanness picks up attachments and beliefs that pull one away from that pure spiritual essence; therefore, more lifetimes come to heal and enlighten that which happened. The changing needs of the human part and the soul part have dictated whether it's been in partnership or not.

Cathy: If at the soul level there is a particular intention that is best served by being single, and at the level of the personality there's an intention to find a partner, then do the soul's intentions always override the desires of the personality?

Council: No; the agreement happens with the soul: 'You can have this now; we'll do this work later. You can have the human satisfaction now.'

Cathy: What is someone to think who reads this chapter who may have been single many years against their conscious desire?

Council: It depends on the person and where they are in their journey of evolution. It could be that their soul is guiding them in a stronger way. It could be that their humanness feels unworthy and is keeping them from it. It could be a number of things for each person. And so, each person would do well to ask themselves where the flow of life and the openness of their heart and the connection with their humanness and their soul's purpose are merging. Look clearly at the intention of the soul and the humanness and see where the merge is or is not happening or could be fostered.

Cathy: What are some other reasons souls plan before coming into body to be single for many years or an entire lifetime?

Council: A fostering of faith. A reaching out to connect with and recognize the Divine inside. There are ways of knowing one's Self that can be fulfilled more clearly when a person is on their own.

Cathy: Many people have spiritual practices to remember their inner Divinity, but they're still lonely and want to have a partner. What would the Council say to those people?

Council: Ask if there is a bigger purpose being served by being single. Ask if you really believe you are worthy of a relationship and of being loved. Do you love yourself deeply and completely? Are you ready to receive as well as give love?

Cathy: How would someone who is single know if that's part of the plan because it serves their highest good or if they're single because somehow they've gotten off track?

Council: The feeling of purity and clarity will be more easily discerned when it's part of the plan. When a person is off track, there is much more confusion and not knowing how to find their way. Things will not make sense.

Cathy: I felt compatible with Jim, that he could have been a good partner, and that if I had married him, I would have had a very different life. Was that a specific option in my pre-birth plan?

Council: Yes. That path could perhaps have been more humanly fulfilling, with love, comfort, and more financial security in the world. You could have chosen that and still done growth work. It would have looked different. It may not have been as spiritually deep unless Jim had made a choice to join you in your spiritual endeavors, which was a possibility. That would have been his choice to make.

Cathy: If I felt before birth that healing and learning could best be accomplished not being in a relationship, then why even plan that option with Jim at all?

Council: We expected this question from Rob.
[laughing]

   You like to look at life from many sides and make choices from an informed place. You appreciate concepts and often don't make decisions until you know how they feel. It suited you to lay out a choice, a fork in the road. Had you been more mature and humanly evolved at the time of the relationship with Jim, you could have very well chosen that path, had a very good, fulfilling life, and then done the spiritual journey in another life. When Jim came into your life, you were unskilled in, and had a superficial understanding of, relationships. You did not have enough of you to bring forward.

Cathy: I'd like to ask now about Star Heart. Is he a soulmate?

Council: Yes. You understand clearly that your souls have journeyed together for eons. You have helped and supported each other. In this current lifetime he has watched over and protected you but kept enough distance to allow you to walk on your own.

Cathy: What is a soulmate?

Council: In the human world, there is confusion about the term. Some think of a soulmate as romantic perfection. This is one way of looking at soulmates. Others recognize walking side by side through lifetimes, looking after each other, helping each other grow, or playing a role for each other.

A soulmate may never incarnate in the same lifetime. It is like being classmates going through evolution together. Soulmates can choose life forms in different ways, including the ones just described.

Cathy: Does everyone have a soulmate?

Council: Everyone has a soulmate, and it may not be just one.

Cathy: What else can you say to help someone who is struggling with being single see greater meaning or purpose in the experience?

Council: It is always wise and helpful to treat oneself tenderly with love and compassion and to look lovingly within for your own worth, strength, and spark of God. Then watch angst melt away as you develop your own richness. Also, examine the reason why you feel so strongly about having a love relationship. Is it to quell loneliness? To fill a hole? To do deep growth work? Is it for a functional partner or an intellectual companion?

Then piece the two together and see what you come up with. See what you recognize about yourself that can bring you comfort or a path to lead yourself closer to your dreams.

Having prompted Cathy to ask all the questions she and I had, I asked her to thank the Council, the Light Being who had brought her to the Council, Star Heart, Curt, and everyone who had participated in the session in any way for all the wisdom and love they had shared with us, then instructed her to remember the experience. I then counted slowly from one to ten, asking Cathy to return to wakeful consciousness at the count of ten. We sat in silence for a few moments as Cathy oriented herself.

"What was it like to experience the three lifetimes?" I asked when I sensed she was ready to discuss.

"The first was joyful, lovely, and felt like home. It has clearly never left me and has informed me forever. The second had that sense of home again. There was the challenge of being human, too, but it wasn't difficult. It was a flow and a rhythm. It was like, 'See, here's what's possible.' No wonder I'm always longing for that quality in this life! The third showed me the contrast when I make choices that don't reflect the highest truth of me."

"What was it like to talk with the Light Being?"

"It was like talking to the brother I never had. There was this feeling of being chums and also of a wise teacher, a guru—a respected, revered person—but it wasn't in a hierarchical way. It was in a comforting, colleague, team member, helpful way. Sometimes, when I've been in India and have been able to sit with wise masters, some of them have been lofty and removed but some of them just put you at ease. That's how it was. There was a feeling of grace there."

"Cathy, what was it like to talk with the Council?"

"They kept their individuality out of it in order to keep the flow, the essence, of their answers coming in together [from several of them] as one answer. It took a little crafting. It started as a trickle and then gained momentum. At the end when you were saying to thank everybody, I was also thanking you, Rob."

〜

As the adage goes, where you stand depends upon where you sit. If you are a human who "sits" in the third dimension, then your stand on being single for the vast majority of an incarnation may be that such an experience is unwanted, undesirable, and likely lonely and perhaps even painful. If you are a soul who "sits" in the nonphysical realm, then your stand on decades of being single may well be that it represents a magnificent and indeed unique opportunity for expansion, healing, and the acquisition of wisdom. Here we have two diametrically opposed viewpoints, and both are correct from the perspective of the observer. The former leads to resistance and suffering, the latter to acceptance and peace. A central tenet of this book is that we can shift from the limited vantage point of the human to the much more elevated perspective of the soul. Doing so immensely eases the human journey and empowers us to learn its underlying lessons in a more conscious and less arduous manner.

A soul having a human experience is subject to profound and often imperceptible conditioning. We accommodate to and stop noticing that which is ever present, and conditioning is present from early childhood and continues throughout a lifetime. Though generally well intentioned, parents, teachers, media figures, and many others extoll the virtues of romantic partnership. Popular media romanticizes romance, making its absence seem unnatural and bleak.

To plan before birth to swim "upstream" against this current of conditioning is an act of boldness and courage. Before we come into body, we choose the time and location of our birth. In our pre-birth planning, we are shown scenes of what society is like at the time and location we have chosen. Cathy well knew that she was incarnating into a society virtually obsessed with romance.

Behind the veil and in a state of self-selected, self-induced amnesia, Cathy spent years forgetful of her true nature. Human need and codependency took the place of unconditional love of self and seeming others; periods of deep longing and loneliness substituted for the soul's knowing of its inherent wholeness and oneness with All That Is. Why would any soul aware of itself as love choose to play a role on a stage in which it forgets its divinity as well as the holiness of all the other actors?

The process of forgetting and then remembering who we really are leads to a more profound self-knowing. During the long periods in which she was not in a romantic relationship, Cathy took the heroine's journey inward to herself. Whether through ceremony, meditation, or just sitting under a tree and being fully present, Cathy remembered her innate beauty, her deeply loving nature, and her sacredness, a sacredness that blesses all who share the Earth with her.

The absence of romantic partnership throughout most of her life provided Cathy with both the opportunity and motivation to, as Aaron put it, "open with love to yourself." One of her pre-birth intentions was to learn how to love and accept herself, for if we cannot fully love and accept ourselves, then we cannot fully receive love and acceptance from others. We receive what we give, and the world mirrors our giving to us. If you ponder why others judge, reject, or fail to appreciate you, ask: In what ways do I judge, reject, or fail to appreciate myself? Then forgive, thank, and bless the people, the triggers who mirrored you to yourself. Earth is a school in which reflectance is our teacher.

Although it is deeply healing to forgive others, *self*-forgiveness is the true midwife of self-love. As Aaron told us, "Until we can forgive ourselves literally for our humanness, we cannot fully love ourselves." Self-blame, the opposite of self-forgiveness, creates an energetic armoring that holds others at a distance. And the old soul keeps inviting not a loving partner but rather one who brings up the self-blame, because there is an intention at the soul level to find compassion for self, compassion that would, in turn, dissolve the armoring.

Too, as The Divine Mother told Cathy, it has been difficult for her to accept love from a partner because she has been afraid of what would be asked of her. Here again relationship with self is the touchstone. As Cathy continues the spiritual journey inward without the distraction of a romantic relationship, she will eventually, whether in this lifetime or another, cultivate abundant self-love. Once she knows that she loves herself, she will trust herself to always act for her highest good, which in part means that she will not place excessive demands upon herself. That vibration will then magnetize to her a partner who can be trusted not to ask too much of her.

As Aaron told Cathy, "The deeper relationship is not the primary thing you wanted. The growth of the soul is." When that growth was best facilitated by being in relationship, Cathy had a romantic partner. Through those relationships she learned that it is wise not to try to fix someone and that she has the strength to say no *with lovingkindness* to negativity. When her growth was best accomplished by being single, Cathy did not have a partner. During those times she traveled inward, fostered her faith, and rediscovered the Divine within. Though not without its share of struggle and pain, her journey was perfect for her in each *now* moment, giving her exactly what she most needed, if not what she most wanted.

Through the eyes of the soul do we see that perfection.

CHAPTER 5

⚭

Celibate Relationships

OVERLIGHTING IS A PHENOMENON IN which a nonphysical being—a spirit guide, for example—envelopes within its energy body a physical being such as a human. Because the nonphysical being is at a higher vibration, the person being enveloped feels a distinct uplift in energy. Essentially, the human is now wrapped in a warm blanket of love. Feelings of joy, peace, and even bliss may occur. A shift in perception may also take place: the person now looks at the world through more loving eyes.

I experienced overlighting at the beginning and throughout much of my conversation with Sarah, who had agreed to share the story of her celibate but loving marriage with Jim. Although I had never experienced overlighting, I knew immediately what was happening. Spirit was saying to me: *Sarah's story is important. We suggest you put it in your book.* I also understood intuitively why Spirit felt this way: celibate relationships (where celibacy is defined as an absence of intercourse) are common and often quite love filled, yet those in such relationships struggle with self-judgments about normalcy.

Sarah and Jim married when both were forty-eight years of age. Although they genuinely love and respect each other, and although both feel the marriage is right for them, their celibacy is an issue Sarah feels has never been properly addressed.

As Sarah and I began our conversation, and as I bathed in the beautiful, almost intoxicating energy of the being who was over-lighting me, I already knew from Spirit's loving nudge that Sarah and Jim had mutually agreed upon the celibacy before either was born. Yet, why would any couple want to experience such a challenge, particularly one that is so often judged by society as "abnormal"? What lessons or healing could emerge from this form of suffering? I was eager to see where Spirit would lead us.

Sarah

Sarah was sixty-two at the time of our conversation. The mid-dle child of eleven in an Irish Catholic family, there was "lots of love in the house," she told me, "along with my big secret, which was being sexually molested by my older brother Steve for most of my childhood. I'm lucky and grateful that I had seven brothers, all of whom but one were appropriately affectionate. My father was warm, always appropriate, and supportive mostly." So, there was a combination of a great deal of love and a great deal of trial with her family of origin.

"I work in marketing at a large corporation in New York City. My husband, Jim, also works there. We work in different parts of the company, but we have some crossover projects. It's nice; we understand each other's business and have a great deal in common."

Sarah and Jim met through her work with various branches of the company around the U.S. Jim was a well-known market-ing executive at one of those branches. His work received many awards, and he was admired by those in his field.

"The spark of attraction for Jim started at a conference we have every summer," Sarah remembered. "All the marketing people from all the branches come together. There's a party at the end of the conference. Every year, even when we didn't know each other very well, Jim made a beeline for me to ask me to dance.

"An interesting fact about Jim is that he's half African American and half Japanese. So, he's very striking and different.

I'm this Irish Catholic girl with strawberry blonde hair—always the life of the party.

"Anyway, at this party we were dancing. All of sudden I realized just how hot he was. I thought, *Oooh, it feels good to be dancing with him!* He's muscular; his arms were a turn on."

Sarah and Jim continued getting together when he came to New York on business. On each trip he invited Sarah to lunch. Finally, for the fifth date he asked her to dinner.

"By this point I was wearing a sign that said, '*It's OK to kiss me*,'" Sarah laughed. As she and Jim rode the subway to their dinner destination, she snuggled next to him to show her interest. After dinner, as they walked downtown, Jim took her hand. "That's when I knew we were going to be an 'item,'" she said. And then it happened: their first kiss.

"We were in Greenwich Village, looking in store windows, just strolling," Sarah reminisced. "I stood on a high step. When I turned around, he finally kissed me for the first time. When Jim tells the story, he talks about how my hair was backlit. He's so cinematic! I said, 'Well, it's about time!' Then we walked more. After a while we were sitting on a park bench. It was so romantic. I said, 'Why do you think neither of us has ever been married?' He said, 'So that we could be sitting on this park bench together right now.' I was smitten!"

Shortly after they started dating, Sarah and Jim learned they had grown up in upstate New York in homes just a three-minute drive from each other. They took a day trip to show each other those homes. As they drove Sarah shared with Jim her fond memories of the skating rink near her family's home where she had learned to skate. She told him how she loved to hear the Beatles' song "Nowhere Man" play as she skated. Just a few seconds later, "Nowhere Man" came on their car radio. Sarah and Jim were stunned. "Jim was so freaked out by that!" Sarah told me. "We were getting signs from the Universe."

Not long after the first kiss, Sarah and Jim became intimate. "We made love almost every day," she said. "But there was a part of me I was reserving. I had self-esteem issues because of the sexual abuse. I was afraid that if I showed all of myself to Jim during our courtship, he wouldn't want me."

At Christmas four months after their first kiss, Jim came to New York for two weeks to visit Sarah. On Christmas Eve he told her that something was wrong with a large, animated billboard in Times Square—a billboard for which he was responsible in his job—and that he would have to look at it. He persuaded Sarah to join him.

"I was trying to help find out what the problem was," Sarah recounted, "and all of a sudden my face came up on the billboard as big as two houses! Then a poem he had written for me scrolled on the screen. I thought, *This is amazing!* The whole, beautiful poem goes on and on until at the end, 'Sarah, will you marry me?' in letters as big as a building! I immediately said yes. He had the ring right there.

"That Christmas was heavenly. Throughout all of this time our sexual life was very loving. It was like a dream of sexual love, but the sex itself was not always in sync. But I figured it didn't matter because we were at just the beginning of our relationship."

One of the ways in which they were out of sync was that Jim wanted to penetrate Sarah without much foreplay. Too, Jim wanted Sarah to climax many times. Sarah felt that Jim was trying to perform for her, and she felt pressure to perform for him. She was hesitant to discuss her concerns. When she did, she felt he took her comments the wrong way.

"There was a combination of my fear at talking openly about these things," Sarah acknowledged, "and his crazy overreaction when I would mention anything. I felt I had to be so careful. He'd say, 'How do you think I feel when you say I'm not pleasing you?' Both of us were so overly sensitive. This is one of the ways in which we are so alike and so well suited, but our heightened sensitivity makes it harder to communicate.

"Also, as soon as he came, it was over for him. Then after a while it became difficult and frustrating for him, because even though he wanted to make love to me for a couple of hours, he really didn't have the stamina for it anymore. All that happened even before we were married."

The wedding day came, and Sarah and Jim exchanged vows in a beautiful ceremony. They made love that night and every night of their honeymoon—until the last night. Earlier that day they argued about money. On the flight home Jim didn't speak to Sarah. After they returned home, Jim fell into a depression. Then, for the first six months after their honeymoon, they had no sex at all.

Sarah told Jim, "You got married for a reason. Part of that reason is to show another human being what it's sometimes like for you. You don't have to go through this by yourself. I'm here. I'm not going anywhere."

Jim saw a doctor. The medication he received helped him to emerge from the depression, but it also diminished his libido. Sarah and Jim started to make love again. At first it was once every few weeks. "Then it became every three, four, six months," Sarah said sadly. "I really don't know when it stopped. I felt awful, betrayed. I thought I was finally going to have a wonderful sexual relationship with a man I adore, and yet this was one of the worst sex experiences of my life. And here it was my husband!" I heard the pain in her voice as she spoke.

Over time Sarah came to realize that it was not helpful to be constantly upset about the lack of sex. She joined a woman's support group, which helped her to take the focus off Jim and put it instead on making herself happy. A friend emphasized the importance of being authentic, particularly in regard to expressing affection when she felt affectionate.

"That led to a lovely, relaxed opening up of sexual affection that persists and flowers to this day," Sarah said more happily. "We hold hands when we watch a movie. We hug in the house. We kiss. We fondle each other sexually—not to the point of orgasm, but often involving arousal. We've said to each other that we are committed to rejuvenating our sensual life, but to this point in time it hasn't happened."

"Sarah, how long has it been since the lovemaking stopped?" I asked.

"Gosh, I've blocked it out, Rob. It's years. It's sad, but I still feel hopeful. The fact that we are affectionate, loving, and sensual on a daily basis keeps it lively enough so that I don't feel unloved or unwanted. It feels like how people are when they're old."

Part of the difficulty for Sarah and Jim is that they sleep in separate bedrooms. Jim, who is a light sleeper, needs to do so to sleep well, which, in turn, helps to keep the depression at bay. On weekdays Sarah and Jim leave home early and come home late, by which time neither has the energy to initiate sex. "My thought now," Sarah said, "and I've asked Jim for this, is 'Let's sleep together just one or two nights a week.' He said, 'That could work.' But we've never actually done it, because really we're both afraid."

On occasion Sarah has tried dressing up in costumes to jump-start their sex life. At times Jim liked this. At other times he responded with irritation or anger, particularly when feeling depressed, saying, "Now that means I have to have sex with you?"

"I was getting all these mixed messages," Sarah recalled. "So now I have these little costumes and I want to put them on, but I'm afraid of rejection."

"Let's talk about this now from a pre-birth planning perspective," I suggested. "Do you believe that you and Jim planned for it to be this way?"

"I do, because it's such a powerful thing in our lives that it has to be something we planned."

"Why do you believe you and Jim planned it?"

"Jim needs to learn to integrate love and sex," Sarah explained. "In his sexual life before me, he was insatiable. There was a lot of experimentation, lots of women. He's learning that there's love without sex. Also, Jim's overarching life challenge is to feel a sense of belonging." Here Sarah was referring to Jim's mixed ethnicity. "This is probably the first time in his entire life that he feels that. If he could integrate the sense of belonging he feels with me and the love he has for me into sexual expression, that would be very satisfying for him. For me, I need to learn that there can be sex with love. It's knowing my essential value—being able to love myself, believe that I'm lovable, and experience myself as a beloved creature of God."

I asked Sarah to say more about how she feels the absence of sex can help her to grow.

"This [relationship] is the last holdout for me. In all my other relationships I can be totally myself and say what I really think. I still can't do that, or I still somehow don't choose to do that, with Jim. It's like there's too much at stake. My desire is to get over that. I'm always reminding myself to say what I really think. It's like the habit of hiding that came from my sexual molestation, feeling not worthy, less than. I don't want to have that habit anymore. I'd like to be completely open in the relationship that is the most challenging, the arena of experience that is the most difficult and most rewarding. The thing in my life that I'm the proudest of is that I've managed to turn what was a very unhappy marriage into a very happy marriage—sex or no sex. That's an accomplishment on a soul level that I can take with me no matter what happens."

As Sarah spoke, I reminded myself that we call relationships to ourselves for healing and expansion. In Jim she had found the perfect partner to heal the wounds of her childhood molestation and expand into the self-love her soul wishes her to know.

"Sarah, there will be people who read your story who have no or infrequent sex in their relationship, but they love their partner and want the relationship to be as happy and loving as it can be. What words of wisdom would you offer to them?"

"First and most important, do not blame your partner. Whenever we blame, it's usually because there's something in us we're not focusing on. First look to yourself. Explore your own sensuality in your own time. I would encourage self-pleasuring. I'll tell you a secret. In times when I was exploring my own sensuality and self-pleasuring on a regular basis, those were the times when my husband came around and wanted to have sex with me. It's because self-love is attractive. If you're not thinking well of yourself, your partner sometimes will believe you and will start to treat you not so well. It helps to treat yourself well."

Here we had come to an important and fundamental truth about life: The Universe mirrors us to ourselves. When we are loving to ourselves, that is reflected to us in our relationships. When we are unloving to ourselves, that, too, is mirrored to us by how others treat us.

"Sarah, you talked about the importance of not blaming one's partner. What would you say to people who blame or judge themselves?"

"Focus on the bigger picture," she advised. "We are in these situations because of something we want to learn as souls. Search your heart for the reasons why this is valuable. There's something very important for you to do on your own while you're in the safety and blessing of that partnership. There aren't rules. People have a picture about the way marriage should be, but there are an infinite number of ways a soul can express itself. Marriage is a vehicle. The way your soul decides to express itself in marriage may be very different from the picture that society—you know, Prince Charming and Cinderella—puts out there. I look at it from a perspective of more than one lifetime. That's the quickest way to get to a point where you are happy together regardless of the circumstances because you're journeying together. And regardless of how much of the journey you share with each other, you're sharing all of it on a soul level. I sometimes talk to Jim's soul. *'Hey, Jim's soul on the other side of the veil, I just want you to know how much I love you and want to be open and honest with you in this life.'* I swear that helps sometimes."

"Sarah, let's say that some people reading your story have adopted society's view that we are supposed to have sex with a certain frequency in a relationship. They feel there's something wrong, bad, or abnormal about their relationships because they're not doing that. What would you say to them?"

"If you have a child or friend who's telling themselves there is something bad or wrong with their relationship because they aren't having sex enough, you would look at them and see their beauty. In fact, you would see the beauty of both people and know in your heart that they're traveling their path the way they should. So, I would encourage that person to look for and create the meaning. Accept the experience and try to see what it's teaching you. If you resist it, you'll learn nothing and make it worse, but if you open your mind and heart to yourself and your partner, you will stand a much better chance of experiencing what was meant to come true for you."

Sarah's Between Lives Soul Regression

With courage and honesty, Sarah had shared with me both her love for Jim and the pain she feels in regard to their celibacy. Had she planned before she was born to experience this difficult challenge, and if so, why? We began our inquiry into her life blueprint with a BLSR.

I began the session with a prayer, asking Sarah's loved ones, guides, angels, and all in Spirit who love and guide her to join us. I then took Sarah through the usual mental and physical relaxation steps and the past life regression portion of the BLSR. I instructed her to emerge from a tunnel into a significant scene in a significant past life. Then I asked her to describe what she saw.

"I'm outside," she began, "in the countryside, daytime, warm summer. I'm with someone. I have bare feet, a brown, rustic skirt, an apron, and a white, eyelet blouse: everyday peasant clothes."

"Good. Now I want you to see yourself standing in front of a mirror so you can see your face and hair clearly. Describe your face and hair to me."

"Brown hair, long, but not that long. A hooked nose, but attractive. I look a little surprised and scared. I'm female, maybe thirty. I'm white with tan skin. Medium build."

"Allow the mirror to dissolve," I prompted, "then describe to me everything you become aware of and everything you do so I can follow you."

"There's a man with me," Sarah continued. "He's trying to control me in some way that I don't want. I'm subservient to him. He seems to care about me, but he's not aware of how much he hurts me. I matter only in a superficial way to him. He thinks he loves me, but I don't feel loved by him. I think he's my owner. He's not my husband."

"You mentioned that you look surprised and scared," I repeated. "Why is that?"

"There's nobody else but him. We're in a farmyard setting. He just tried to take advantage of me."

"I want you to look closely at this man's face and into his eyes and tell me, do you recognize this soul as anyone who is in your current lifetime?"

"Steve. My brother Steve," Sarah indicated, certainty in her voice.

"Good. Let's allow the scene to continue. What happens next?"

"He tries to convince me to have sex with him. I don't want to at all, but he's much, much bigger than me—very heavyset and strong—and he forces himself on me. Even though I'm crying in pain and terrified, he somehow thinks I like it. He laughs a lot, then closes his pants. I'm on the ground. I push my skirt back over my legs. I'm crying. He says I liked it, and then he leaves."

"How do you feel?"

"I feel terrible," she said, beginning to cry. "I feel hurt, degraded, alone. I feel frightened like he might do it again. I don't feel like there's anybody I can talk to about it."

"I understand. I want you to trust that your soul and guides are showing you this scene for a particular reason. What is important for you to know or understand about the scene you're being shown? Trust that you know the answer."

"I need to understand that it wasn't right," Sarah told me. "And that I was not to blame. I didn't ask for it. I didn't deserve it. Even when I wanted to be attractive, it doesn't mean I should be treated that way."

"Is there more that's important for you to experience in this scene, or do you feel complete and ready to move ahead?"

"I feel complete."

"On the count of three you will automatically move ahead to the next significant event or scene in that same lifetime.

One . . . two . . . and three! Tell me, where are you now, and what is happening?"

"I'm in a small city. I have a hat on and more prosperous cloth-ing. I'm maybe ten years older. I see a carriage. I'm about to get in that carriage when . . . I see him! I wasn't expecting to see him!"

"That same man?"

"Mmm hmm. He's standing in the street, a little ways away from me. He sees me."

"How long has it been since you've seen him?"

"Ten years."

"Do you approach each other?"

"No."

"How do you feel when you see him?"

"Very proud."

"Why do you feel proud?"

"I married someone with position in this small city. He [the rapist] thought I was nothing, but I am not nothing! I'm proud of the fact that I'm valued by another who loves and cares for me and that he [the rapist] no longer has any power over me."

Sarah then told me she was ready to move forward. I advanced her to the next significant scene in that lifetime.

"I'm on my deathbed," she stated. "There's a bright light in the room. I think it's from Spirit. I have family around me, and I'm not afraid. My husband is there, but I can't tell if he's in Spirit or there [in body]. My son who's grown up and his wife are there."

I instructed Sarah to look closely at the faces of all who are there. "Do you recognize any of these souls as people who are with you in your current lifetime?" I asked.

"My son in my past life is my sister, Claire, in this life. His wife is Danny, my sister's boy in this current life."

"Approximately how old are you?"

"Seventy."

"What year is it? See the numbers in your mind."

"1882."

"In what country have you lived most of your life?"

"Austria."

"What is going on around or within you that suggests your physical death will come by day's end?"

"I feel a certainty in my heart."

"How do you feel about this life just lived?"

"I feel that I came a long way," Sarah said with satisfaction. "In the beginning of my life, I was very much alone. I think that's why I chose in this [current] life to be surrounded by so many brothers and sisters. I didn't want to go through that again with no love and support around me. I finally conceived a son later in life, and his wife came to be very good comfort to me as well. He was my only child. I was so happy to finally create a family after being impoverished and unwelcomed. I somehow made my way to a better life. I feel at peace with it and happy that I decided to do it."

I guided Sarah to leave the physical body in the past life.

"Where are you now in relation to your body?" I asked her.

"Above the village. I'm saying goodbye and thank you to my family." She began to cry again.

"Take as much time as you need."

"It's hard to leave," she sighed. And after a few moments, "OK."

"Before we prepare to move farther away from your body and begin your journey back home, is there any unfinished business on Earth you would like to attend to?" I wondered.

"There's something with my husband."

"Go to him now. You have the ability to go to him. What is it you wish to take care of with him?"

"I want to tell him that I'm sorry I didn't fully love him the way he loved me or the way I wished I could have. I want to tell him that I'm grateful for the life he gave me, that I do love him very, very much, that I'm sorry I rejected him physically and that I couldn't receive the pleasure he wanted to give me."

Sarah had not mentioned any of these things in her descriptions of the past life scenes, but their importance was nevertheless clear. I prompted her to travel in her spirit body to her husband in the past life. We paused for a few moments as she did so.

"I've found him," she told me.

"You have the ability to communicate telepathically with him," I guided. "Go ahead now and share with him what you just told me. Take as much time as you need."

"It was Kevin," Sarah stated as she came into a sudden recognition of her past life husband. "Kevin is a man I dated when I was younger in my current life."

"Tell him everything that you would like to. Tell me when you're ready to continue."

After a pause, "I'm ready."

I guided Sarah to move upward away from the Earth plane and back to our nonphysical Home. She told me she saw bright light above her, and I encouraged her to move into the light.

"The first thing I notice," she said, "are pastel blue and pink clouds. I'm moving toward a building with some columns and a round top. There's a little [town] square in front of it. There are a few people there waiting for me. It's my grandmother, my father," (here Sarah burst into tears) "my Uncle Jim, and my mom. My mom is really happy. She's jumping up and down like she really missed me. She's like a little sprite. It's been so long since we've been able to talk! My Uncle Jim is smiling. My grandmother is very important to me."

I told Sarah to take a private moment with her family to thank them for coming, to express her love for them, and to allow them to express their love for her. After a few moments of silence, Sarah then began to relay to me verbatim what her family was telling her. Each time she spoke, she started by telling me who was speaking.

"I really enjoyed being your father," Sarah's father said both to and through her. "It was fun to watch you and play with you, especially when you were little. You were a goofy kid full of energy and intelligence. And you were very demanding."

"When you were a little kid and learning to walk," Sarah's mother chimed in, "I had to give nickels to your brothers to help you. You would grab their fingers and walk and walk and walk. If they got bored and put you down, you would scream" (her mother was laughing now) "until I paid them to walk you again. You were a [spiritual] seeker from your earliest moments as a child. It was my joy to take you around. I would have taken you anywhere. I enjoyed watching you try everything." Sarah cried softly as her mother spoke through her.

"Sarah," I prompted, "I'd like you to ask them why you were shown the particular past life you saw."

"You were shown that lifetime because it has bearing on this [current] life," her grandmother said. "That big man who raped you—in this life you're currently living, he violated you for many years in your childhood, and it got confused. Because it was so much a part of your life, you thought you were responsible. You felt guilty, and that's why you didn't want to tell anyone. It was important to see that other life, because it's a lot easier to see there that what he did was wrong, that you weren't responsible, and that it was a behavior of his and not yours. The similarity in your personality and look—even as a little girl—attracted your brother to do that. But your light is your light; it's not anybody's to put out." With this Sarah cried harder. I paused to give her a moment.

"Sarah," I suggested, "I'd like you to ask your family what your brother is working on in his current lifetime."

"Your brother is working on learning how to take responsibility for who he is and what he does," Sarah's father replied. "He's working on responding to a higher impulse within himself. He is wrestling with this now."

"The bond that brought about that abusive situation is breaking down," Sarah's uncle chimed in. "It was a bond more on your brother's side. He's been fixated on you. You wanted to give him the chance to redeem himself."

Here we had a major revelation. Out of her great love for, and in service to, the soul of her current brother, Sarah had agreed as part of her pre-birth plan to accept the possibility of incest. As souls we are often willing to take such risks to provide our fellow souls with the growth opportunities they need. (I refer readers here to the chapter on incest in my second book, *Your Soul's Gift.*)

Speaking as one, Sarah's family then explained that in the past life Sarah felt guilt for not having sexual relations more often with her husband and as well for feeling attracted to his brother, who is Jim in her current lifetime. Both of these forms of guilt have been carried forward energetically and are now preventing physical intimacy with Jim.

"Sarah," I suggested, "ask your family what specifically you and Jim planned in regard to sex for your current lifetime and why." With this, Sarah announced that Jim's soul was present and wanted to speak through her.

"Both Jim and Sarah wanted to integrate sex and love," said Jim's soul. "Both are scared. Both don't want to feel rejected. Jim loves her. A part of him is finally relaxing enough to feel that love as it is expressed in a daily, mundane way."

"Did Sarah and Jim know before they came into body that they would have this period of years in which they would be mostly sexually inactive?" I asked.

"Absolutely, yes," confirmed Jim's soul. "It's a period of time in his incarnation to change his understanding from pure lust to sexual love and also to gain clarity about what love is. Both Sarah and Jim have had difficulty believing in love from the opposite sex. This has been a theme in many lifetimes. Both have been very able to manipulate the opposite sex. Both have been tough on the opposite sex. They needed to learn that a deep love and marriage could be sustained without sex in order to fully integrate love into the subsequent expression of sexuality."

I asked Jim's soul if Sarah and Jim had learned this lesson fully or if they have more to learn.

"The 'more' is honesty," answered Jim's soul. "They are not dishonest with each other, but they are not as open as they could be. So, the 'more' is sharing and allowing themselves to be completely open to each other. Not just 'I'm going to be open now,' but rather 'I will let the boundaries fall away. I will be completely aware that despite my trepidation, you're the one I wish to be completely open to.' It's different from saying what they think or feel. It's a feeling of no reservation and a deep, abiding trust. They don't have that yet."

"How would Sarah and Jim create this kind of complete openness and trust?" I wondered.

"Keep pushing the boundary little by little so that the openness is real," Jim's soul advised. "If they feel afraid, go toward the love. When they're afraid, think of what's most loving and do that. Jim's desire is to feel deeply lovable and deeply loving in this life."

"So," I said, "the things that are standing in the way of Sarah and Jim having a more active sex life and greater openness and intimacy are the two forms of guilt Sarah carried forward energetically from the past life as well as a mutual fear of disappointing the other?"

"Yes," stated Jim's soul.

"It's important in a relationship to know if you're behaving out of fear or out of love," Sarah's grandmother added. "If you feel fear, just turn that around and ask yourself, 'What is loving in this moment?' and do that instead.

"There are no rules in marriage," she continued. "There's no way it has to be or should be. There's only love. Let that be your guide. When you feel insecure about the lack of sex, remind yourself to go with a more loving thought toward yourself or your husband. As you train yourself to do more loving thinking, that will help."

"Sarah," I asked, "what else can your family tell us about what you and Jim planned before you were born in regard to sex and love?"

"Jim trusted that the relationship was going to be so important to Sarah that she would never, ever, ever give up," Sarah's family said as one. "He knew not only that she would never give up once they found each other, but also that she would never give up on finding him in the first place. Both knew that would take a long time, and that was OK because both knew they had a lot of relationship ground to cover before they got together, because too soon in this lifetime would have resulted in failure. Both had to get to a point where they had enough experience with other people and go through some lessons before they got to each other, where they hoped to learn the ultimate lesson."

"What is the ultimate lesson?" I asked them.

"Loving themselves enough to feel the value they bring so that they're not afraid and that their reactions to each other are not reactions in fear."

"I find that the only time I'm offended or hurt is when I'm not really loving myself," Sarah observed, now speaking as herself. "That's really a big deal to learn. If Jim's thoughtless, that's him. If I choose to be hurt, that's me."

I asked Sarah's family what else she and Jim have to learn about sex and love.

"What they would like to learn about sex and love," answered Sarah's grandmother, "is how to express the full range of crying, joy, depth, intrinsic beauty, and the power of creation that's within love—and that love *is*. They're together to pull the creative power of love from Spirit into body, heal themselves and each other, and bring that power into the world in creative ways they have not yet imagined."

A fundamental principle of Life is that what we focus on increases. When we add love to our focus, we imbue our attention with the transformative power of the Divine. The combination of focus and love blesses and uplifts all. Through their relationship Sarah and Jim were in the process of remembering this power, a power they knew before birth and then chose to forget. As they remember it, they come into a deeper knowing of the power of love, a knowing that would not be possible without the temporary forgetting.

"What does it mean to truly comfort another person?" I then asked Sarah's family. "What is required to do that?"

"The most important requirement," her family said as one, "is to believe in them and reflect to them their ultimate beauty, value, and goodness, and a certain knowledge that all is well and all always will be well. And physical touch is very important: bringing all that creative power of love into your arms and putting those arms around another human."

"I'd like to have the highest vantage point possible," I told them. "What is the role of sex in human romantic relationships? Why are we sexual beings in the first place?"

Sarah then announced that her soul was present and was going to speak through her.

"The primary role of sex is to [help you] remember that you are Spirits, to share an ever-increasing experience of creation itself. Human love is only a small part of All There Is, and All There Is is Love. There's nothing else. So, when you're in the body, it's natural to want to touch a creative source. Since the creative source is Love, your rejoining soul-to-soul in physical life when you meet each other again ignites that spark of Love. You follow that flame like a moth to get to a point where you can touch creation. You're peeling back the edge and experiencing life where it starts, that part between the manifest and unmanifest. So, the purpose of sex is really the highest purpose of life: to express love and to touch the creative source."

"Sarah, when we first asked about the infrequency of sexual relations between you and Jim, we were told that there are no rules, no shoulds," I recalled. "Can Spirit expand upon that?"

"It's very important," advised Sarah's grandmother, "not to get tied up in expecting from your life, yourself, or others the fulfillment of a fantasy. Be in the moment of love. Every moment is either an expression of love or a relative failure of love, since love is all there is."

"Being close to and accepting of your sexual self is a way of being in touch with Spirit," added Sarah's father. "Spirit is love, and the world is physical. So, physical love—sensuality—is the full expression of love in the physical realm."

"We'll need to conclude now," I told Sarah. "I'd like you to take a private moment with everyone who's there and offer your gratitude to them for all the love and wisdom they've shared with you today, and allow them to express their love and gratitude to you. Take as much time as you need. Tell me when you're ready to continue."

"I'm glad to see you all," Sarah said to her family. We paused for a minute as she cried softly. "Thank you for being there for me. I'm ready."

"Before we leave them," I prompted, "I'd like you to ask them to provide you with an energetic healing on all levels: physical, emotional, mental, and spiritual. Tell me what happens next."

"The four of them are now looking more like beings of light," Sarah described. "They're rising up. They're becoming a waterfall of light. The four of them are surrounding my body and pouring that light into me. They form a bullet-shaped capsule around me. I feel my heart opening and receiving. I feel their humor and their love and their joy at being together again and being together with me. I feel my mother and father, that they are so happy together. They're as much a part of each other as they were when they were my parents. I'm feeling both their individuality and their unity with each other and with me. I'm feeling real joy within the wisdom."

The healing now complete, I suggested to Sarah that she would remember all that she had experienced today. I then guided her slowly and gradually out of the trance state and back to a full, waking state. We were silent for a few moments as she reoriented herself.

"Hi Rob; I'm ready," she announced.

"So, what was that like for you?"

"There were several times when I knew that I was receiving advanced or new information that has lived within me but that I hadn't been aware of yet."

"How did you know that?"

"It felt like I was joining with something else. The understanding was partly there within me, but it went beyond my understanding. It was very emotional. I was doing a lot of crying throughout," Sarah said, now laughing. "Even when it didn't seem like I was crying, there were tears coming out.

"When you said the prayer in the beginning, it was like— boom!—they were all there, and they were banging down the door to get in, like they didn't want to wait until the end of the show. Also, it was the emotion of finally being with somebody who could comfort me. It's not as though Jim can't comfort me, but I felt I was with people who completely understood me and were very eager to help."

I asked Sarah what she felt she gained most from the experience.

"The knowledge that there is a real reason for what's going on in my life and my marriage. The idea that there had to be a time of no sex to celebrate the love. In most of Jim's relationships before me, it was all about sex and not as much about love. I think I'm the first person he's ever actually let himself be in love with."

"Sarah, is your understanding of the role of sex in human relationships different as a result of what you heard today?"

"Yes, very much so. I never really focused on physical manifestation of the initial, creative source. It's like taking love from the unmanifest to the manifest. That's the longest 'distance' you can go! So, bringing love all the way out and expressing it in physical form is actually a very spiritual thing. I've given lip service to that, but I never really understood or felt it. Now, I do. I get it more deeply and in a way that really relates to my life in particular."

"Do you have any sense of how your relationship with Jim may be different going forward?"

"There's a comfort level now with this new understanding and reassurance. It gives me a renewed confidence that it's really OK."

"What else do you feel came out of the session for you?"

"In that past life during the rape I did feel pleasure. That was very confusing [to me in that lifetime], because I didn't know anything about sex, and then this man raped me, and in spite of the pain and the fear there was also pleasure mixed in. It made me not want to have sex with my husband, but it also made me want that feeling [of pleasure] that I never allowed myself to have again in that lifetime. So, I think that I'm trying to integrate that experience with Jim so that I can finally have the pleasure along with the love instead of either love and no pleasure or no love and pleasure. I'm trying to get those two things to come together for myself."

"Do you feel that what you learned today will help you to do that?"

"Yes, I do."

Sarah's Session with Pamela and Jeshua

Sarah's Between Lives Soul Regression had given us much insight into Sarah's plan for her current lifetime. To see what else we might learn, Sarah and I spoke with Pamela and Jeshua.

"I'll start with a question," I began. "Did Sarah and Jim plan before they were born to have, or at least a potential to have, a romantic relationship in which there would be very little sexual activity? The broader question is this: Do couples plan this situation, and if so, why?"

Pamela closed her eyes in order to focus on Jeshua. The three of us were silent for a few moments. As always, I awaited Jeshua's presence with anticipation.

"You have a lot of love inside you," Jeshua said to Sarah as he began to speak through Pamela. "There's a big light shining in your heart; however, you are not deeply aware yet of what this light means. In particular, you have a tendency to want to bring other people to the light, to take care of them, but this can lead to losing your central boundaries. Then you become ungrounded, not fully in touch with your own needs and desires. It's important to get back to yourself, become more firmly grounded, and see the relationship you're in from this perspective. Right now there is a kind of entanglement between your [energy] and Jim's energy; you want to take care of him from a deep sense of love and compassion. But sometimes love can become like a burden or too much for the other person, and this can create problems. Is this fair?"

"Yes," Sarah confirmed. "I submit often in my relationship to Jim because it's just easier than to have so much conflict. I really feel submissive. I let go of my desires in favor of Jim's."

"It's not simply submission," Jeshua clarified. "There's a fear of loneliness inside you. You're playing small. You are acting as if this part of you that is submissive is not really you, but still you do it because you're afraid to be alone."

"And this aloneness essentially has to do with embracing your own life," Pamela added. "You are afraid of your own light, meaning your own creative power and also your own masculine energy."

"It's true," Sarah acknowledged. "I don't know how to embrace my power."

"It has become engrained in the feminine consciousness collectively," Jeshua continued, "that as a woman you need to be serving or taking care of other people's needs, especially a man's needs, and so it has become part of the identity of woman. Being in this role of empathy and understanding, being very alert and always absorbing the other person's energy, is keeping women from truly embracing their autonomy, their strength.

"Sexual energy is life energy. Basically, sex is life. It is a deeply creative energy, and it is not only felt in the bedroom when having physical sex. It's a much broader, wider concept. It's about renewal and originality and creation, creating something new. Whenever two people meet and feel this attraction, there's something there to be explored, to be discovered, and this can feel like a magnetic pull between two people. There's an intense desire not just for the physical sensations, but to get to know each other, and through knowing each other both grow. So, the process of entering into a relationship is a deeply creative one. This is what sexuality is really about on a deeper level.

"In your case, Sarah, what you feel is that on a deeper or soul level you and Jim are not walking next to each other. You're on a different path, but you love each other. You want to come together; however, both of you need to face certain issues on your own. Not everything can be shared.

"Whenever there was attraction and intimacy that has become less and less, it's important to address it on the inner level. There are two reasons why it can diminish or go away. One reason can be that either one or both partners are afraid to face their own shadows, which will inevitably come out in a close relationship. When they are unable to deal with this kind of honesty or openness, one or both can shut down and the communication can stop being open and fresh. Then couples can get into certain habits and patterns, and they get by, they survive, but nothing new is really happening.

"There's another reason why the attraction can stop or slowly fade away. Sometimes two souls meet in an Earth life, and they have something special to share. They encourage each other on a deeper level to face certain issues, and also they feel this creative joy together. However, not all these encounters or relationships are meant to last like in a thirty-year marriage. So, sometimes there can also be a natural ending to a relationship because the dynamic that brought two people together has played out. It naturally finishes. Humans think of it as a failure, but from a soul level that's not necessarily the case."

Jeshua's words reminded me of how so much of human life is not what it appears. Where the personality often perceives failure, the soul sees completed growth.

"Sarah," Jeshua added, "you hold back because you see your own power, and you feel it will blow him away if you show the full extent of your light, your wisdom. There's a kind of shyness or modesty about that, but you cannot stop it. You have to show your true self. It's as though you would like to protect him, and then on the other hand this frustrates you, and then you hold in."

I then asked Pamela and Jeshua what specifically Sarah and Jim had planned in regard to sex. We were silent for a moment as Jeshua stepped aside and Pamela accessed one of Sarah's past lives.

"I see a past life in which you and Jim knew each other," Pamela told Sarah. "He was your father. He was very fond of you. In this past life, as a child you were very introverted. You were a dreamer and had a rich inner life, but you kept it to yourself. So, you were a bit withdrawn and shy.

"He always encouraged you. He was more open than you, more in the world so to speak, but he became attached to you. You were very important, like the flower of his life. But later on you felt a bit imprisoned by this father-daughter relationship. At some point when you were a young woman, you wanted to break free from it. At that moment his energy, which was once very warm and loving, became too protective, even dominating and confining.

"You moved away from him. Another man came into your life. Your father didn't like him at all; he was jealous and critical. You felt split inside. There was a loyalty issue.

"Also, in that lifetime you wanted to write. You had a strong connection with a higher energy, guidance. You wanted to bring this information, this wisdom, down and write about it. This is very much connected to what Jeshua referred to as your light. It's about wanting to bring new awareness into society. You did it in the past life, but it was difficult. You got into trouble [with your father].

"In the beginning of that life, you seemed like a timid, introverted, sensitive girl, but in this sensitivity was great potential because you had strong inner visions. Later in this life you wanted to express it, but then your father didn't support you because he didn't know you in this way. So, it ended with very mixed emotions. You always loved him and wanted to have peace between the two of you, but he kept blaming you because you left him."

"It all makes perfect sense," Sarah confirmed. "In this [current] life he keeps giving me all kinds of advice, as if he doesn't think I know how to behave or to succeed."

"I think he knows perfectly well that you're very capable of doing it yourself," Pamela replied, "but I sense he fears that if you know you don't need him, then what will happen? I sense this fear of abandonment, a fear of being left alone."

"But we both have the same fear," Sarah told us. "He's afraid of me abandoning him, and I'm afraid of being lonely without him."

Pamela then informed us that Jeshua wanted to speak again.

"Your soul wanted to meet him again in this life," he informed Sarah. "At first you gave each other a sense of warmth, tenderness, and belonging. But then you gradually got into this old pattern again, which often happens when something is not resolved in a past life. It will repeat itself because you want to solve it. 'Solve it' means solve it for yourself. You can't solve everything together. Your path is your own. Your soul wants you in this life to address your unique light.

"Also, [your soul wants you to address] what it means that you confront people, that you are not conventional, that you say things that some people may be scared of or resist. This is what your soul wants, and also to be free of this collective feminine submissiveness."

"What's so interesting," Sarah replied, "is that Jim and I are involved in a program, Women's Empowerment and Gender Understanding, we started with the company. We're teaching classes to men and women about gender understanding. I'm trying to get to the other side of that in this life, being myself fully and breaking free from this pattern of letting him, in particular, take over. But I need to be careful and do it gently so that he knows I'm not doing anything against him, because that's how he often perceives it."

"In a way you're not being honest," Jeshua pointed out, "because a part of you is submitting. At a deep level you have certain judgments about Jim, and this part you hold back to keep peace; however, he senses it, and it makes him insecure. From this insecurity he can start to act in a way that's not nice or becomes critical or dominating. You must face this underlying issue yourself. Your position is not clear; it's ambiguous. You should take up your power and see what happens. You cannot control what will happen to the relationship, but your most important mission from the soul's perspective is to embrace this power, this light, your inspiration, to really express yourself and not be held back by this collective feminine disempowerment."

"Sarah, when you and Jim argue," Pamela said, now speaking in her own cadence and tone, "are you afraid to become angry at a moment like that?"

"Very," she confirmed. "I'm terrified. Right away he'll say things like, 'I can't live like this' or 'I'm not going to be in a marriage where we fight.' He's said that to me on more than one occasion. He grew up [in a home] where his parents were always bickering, and he's not going to do it. I know he's not going to leave me, but I have no tolerance for fighting. I need to figure out how to say things so that it can get through to him."

"But in this particular example, he gets upset and feels free to express it to you," Pamela said. "You then take responsibility for his fear of bickering and yours as well. You take the whole load, and then you decide, 'I will keep my voice low.' This will help maybe in the short term but not in the long term because you keep this inside."

With that, Pamela's consciousness stepped aside, and Jeshua returned.

"Just be angry," he advised.

"Oh, my god, that is so scary to me!" Sarah began to cry. "And I know it's . . . I know it's scary to most women."

"Can you explain why it's so scary?" Jeshua asked gently.

"It's fear of loneliness. I'll be in it by myself if I'm so angry that he shuts down, because that's what he always does. If I'm angry, he can't stand it."

"You are lonely now in this relationship," Jeshua observed. "But the most basic loneliness is lack of connection with yourself, your true self, your soul, your inspiration, your intuition. The moment you play small and try to keep the peace, you are dishonest with yourself and the situation. This, too, can create a sense of loneliness, and it's much worse than actually being alone."

"That's true. I'm lonely now whenever I don't say what I truly think, and I feel connected to Jim when I do say what I truly think."

"This is about courage," Jeshua told Sarah. "This whole issue is about courage, because you already know everything [you need to do]."

"You want to hear something funny? One of the exercises I do with the women in my class is called The Courage Finder," Sarah said with a laugh.

"The issue of male dominance is very important; however, it has two sides," Jeshua stated. "In the past, women were rendered powerless because of the roles they had to fulfill, like mother and wife. They couldn't express themselves publicly. However, men were also severely restricted in self-expression. They were allowed—or it was their duty—to work, earn, fight in the army, go to war. All these typical male roles were not really so liberating for men. So, even though they were the dominant gender, that doesn't mean their inner selves or souls were nurtured by the roles they had to fulfill. Men have been cut off from their feelings—their hearts—which is an essential instrument to connect with the soul.

"Both men and women have suffered greatly, and still do, from these very restricted roles. It is time now to break free from these roles, because this is the only way both men and women can get in deeper touch with their souls' essence, with their unique individual soul energy. The moment you identify yourself too strongly with either a masculine or a feminine role as traditionally defined, you limit your soul's expressive power. This goes for both men and women.

"It's important that women understand their role nowadays," he continued. "If they identify too much with being the victim of men and get into a state of anger and frustration about that, it won't be the right dynamic to solve the issue because men have been wounded as well. When men shut down or are emotionally blocked, or when they become aggressive or frustrated because of the demands put on them in relationships, it's very important that women see and start to understand the history of the collective energy of men. Women have a leading role to play here. Only in this way can women create a bridge of healing between the genders."

"How does this affect the sexual relationship for me and for others?" Sarah asked.

"Needing each other sexually should be an expression of the soul's desire for connection and joy," Jeshua answered, "and the traditional roles prescribed to men and women should be let go. It should be more about the individuals' expression and really connecting, communicating at a very intimate level. Sexuality has become so deeply intertwined with power and abuse of power. There is a lot of emotional trauma connected with sexuality. Communication is the key in this area.

"Also, it's important for women to mature, to grow out of this victim or blaming role, and really take up their own creative power. Then there will be a rebirth of the feminine energy in women, and it will naturally integrate with the masculine aspect, which is also in women. So, you are both. When this natural integration happens in women, they will become more independent and autonomous, and their relationship with men will become much less stressed. There will be fewer expectations. Women will in a way set men free to be who they are; no longer will they have to fulfill an archetypical role. Then men will be free to be the individuals they are, just like the women themselves."

I interrupted. "I want to come back to the central question I think we've partially answered: Why are Sarah and Jim not sexually active together? Was this planned before birth, and if so, why?"

"There was a strong attraction in the beginning, a recognition of souls," stated Jeshua. "Part of their intention was that the struggle or conflict they faced in the past life would be reenacted and that they would now choose a more liberating way out. Sarah, your soul wanted to be faced with this issue in order to be liberated from very old-seated fears: the fear of self-expression, in particular the fear of self-expression as a woman. You planned to face this issue. The issue of sexual intimacy is really secondary to the issue of how you relate to each other overall. It is not a self-standing issue; it has to do with the whole relationship dynamic.

"You should decide, Sarah, after going deep inside yourself, if what is happening between the two of you is a temporary phase or if the dynamic has reached a natural end. But I cannot say this to you; it is part of your process to find out for yourself."

"Jeshua, what else can you advise Sarah and Jim regarding how to approach their sexual life now?" I asked. "How can they rejuvenate it? In particular, how would you advise them to handle any sadness, fear, or judgment of themselves or of each other?"

"If you both really want to work on it, you have to be open," he advised Sarah. "You shouldn't be *too* considerate of his feelings, because then you are blocking yourself from self-expression, and this will not help the relationship. Be open even with the raw emotions. Then you regard him as equal. The basic issue is emotional, not sexual, but emotions guide sexuality. Feeling attraction or physical excitement is not a process that is independent; it's quite linked to the emotions.

"Sexuality is so direct, so instinctual, that you cannot hide in this area. If you try, for instance, to keep the peace throughout the day, your energy gets locked up. You're not spontaneous anymore, and so the sex will also not be spontaneous when both have pent-up emotions. Your own sexuality, Sarah, gets stuck in this way. If you refuse to really open up on a raw, emotional level, like really get angry, then what is in the anger *is* your sexual energy. It's your sensuality, your fire, your passion. If you consistently push it away because of wanting to keep peace or being very responsible or saving him, then you repress your own sexual energy, which is creative energy. Sexual energy is the soul's energy, too. It's not independent of it."

"My sexual energy got me into deep trouble as a child," Sarah said sadly.

"Yes, I see this," Pamela said, now speaking as herself. She was tuning into the energy of Sarah's childhood sexual abuse. "I see you're like a dark cloud. This is your anger, your frustration, but there are prison bars around it, very old prison bars. You had the experience of not being able to express it, but I must say in this particular relationship with Jim, your karmic memory, your soul's memory, is that you could not express yourself freely in the past life. So, you have a memory that you can't really be yourself with him. It could be hard in any circumstance to let out raw emotion, but with him there's an extra charge because of the karmic history."

"I'd like to ask Jeshua to speak to the readers now," I said. "What would you say to people who are in a committed relationship in which there's little or no sex?"

"Investigate the reasons why and be open to each other without judgment," he suggested. "Sexuality and intimacy are surrounded by [feelings of] shame, failure, and not being good enough. It's a very delicate issue. The first step that two partners should take is to decide to really address and recognize that each of them is in a lot of pain.

"Recognize that a sexual issue has to do with the whole of a person's energy. It's not a separate part. It has to do with your life energy—being comfortable with yourself, with your truest, unique energy. That's why sexuality is deeply important: it's connected with the soul's expression.

"The moment you feel that your sexual energy is blocked— and this happens for so, so many people—then there's something going on inside. It's important to get into that, both together and personally for yourself. The first step is openness and releasing judgments, and to connect on the soul level. Don't just see each other as man and woman but connect on a level that goes beyond this. Share together as human beings, like friends would, so you can come together more.

"Do not address this issue purely at the physical level. Really address the everyday life: how you interact; how you speak together; what are your hopes, your wishes, your desires. Often when people have been together for a long time they are so used to the patterns that have arisen. Everyday life can also be very busy, and they're absorbed by many things.

"So, it's important that a relationship should never become a habit, because then the sparkle of wonder, excitement, and curiosity will get buried. There will be a lot of dust on it, and the sexual fire will dwindle. So—and this is important in all life— ask yourself what meaning are you really experiencing in what you do, because your greatest gift is your soul's fire, your soul's passion in anything you do."

"Jeshua, how can couples create emotional intimacy without sex?" I wondered.

"Openness is a key. Intimacy. Intimacy means that you are so relaxed with someone that you allow yourself spontaneously to share your deepest feelings. You're not afraid of judgment. The two energy fields of people who are intimate emotionally open up to each other in a very loving way. They truly have this sense of wonder and curiosity about each other instead of looking at each other through the glasses of convention or classifying the other person as successful or rich or this or that. All these general judgments go.

"It's a miracle! When people meet in intimacy, they open up a dimension of true wonder and really seeing each other fresh and new. It takes effort to achieve this, because people are generally easily caught by fear and then mental energy wanting to control and make things work. So, intimacy always requires that you let go of the future to be present in the now. You let go of all controlling mechanisms. For instance, in a marriage you have to be together, you have to do certain things together. There are so many rules and expectations that kill this open sense of wanting to know each other, where are you now, what are you feeling now. This often gets lost along the way. So, people need to create room for that and experience the wonder of it.

"If you want to be intimate, whether you do it to rejuvenate sexual intimacy or are just with a friend, intimacy always requires courage to open up and to lose your fear of the other person's possible rejection or judgment. Intimacy is a big step. It's taking a risk."

"Jeshua, what is the role of sex in human relationships?" I asked. "Why are we sexual beings in the first place?"

"Sexuality is very much misunderstood in society," he observed. "It's because of the scientific paradigm that is now dominant for you. You regard sexuality as a biological mechanism for survival, but the true nature of sexuality is much more sophisticated and more connected with the soul.

"The soul wants to grow, gain more self-knowledge and experience, and open up through relationships. You meet another person, and in that meeting you are confronted with yourself, but in a joyful manner the other person can help you see yourself differently. Both light and shadow parts are deeply present in the dance of a relationship. It's a powerful means of growth. Really, sexuality is the joy of creativity. From the soul's perspective it's not primarily meant for survival. That's why it doesn't matter to the soul whether you are in a homosexual or heterosexual relationship. The basic meaning is the dance of life. Sexuality has to do with celebrating your own uniqueness and sharing it with someone else.

"A deep connection occurs between two individuals when they connect on all levels, meaning both physically and emotionally. This creates a kind of magic between two individuals, which enhances their growth but also impacts the world around them. Sexuality is magical in that it attracts a deeply creative energy. It's a basic source of inspiration for people; however, sexuality is more than just a relationship between two people. Whenever, for instance, an artist feels truly inspired, a painter or writer or whatever she is doing, there's actually a sexual flow into this sense of integration and excitement. Creative inspiration is sexual in nature. So, it's important to see the realm of the sexual not as limited to just the physical or having children."

"Can you go into that deeper?" Sarah requested.

"When you are deeply creative or inspired, it's the highest energy level, the crown chakra," Jeshua told us. "It calls in a circle connected with your root chakra at the base of your spine. It's an energetic happening. It starts to flow up and down. In some traditions this is called a kundalini experience.

"When all levels inside you become involved, and the soul truly mixes with your body and emotional energy, it becomes like a light, a fire, flowing through you. The soul comes down in the higher chakras, down the head, the heart, and then it wants to flow down to the lower energy centers. The abdomen and the root chakra are main blockages because people in the past have been discouraged from truly expressing their creativity. It has to do with history and how people were ruled by institutions, this whole division between men and women in the past, how they were constricted to very limiting roles. This is part of the reason why people have such trouble allowing their creativity, which is also allowing their wholeness, their sexuality, to flow freely. So, it's a much deeper issue than just relationships. It's about becoming free—really free—to express yourself."

Jeshua then stepped aside so Pamela could comment. "When we integrate individually," she added, "when a woman integrates her masculine energy and a man does with his feminine energy, then we become truly creative and our relationship will flourish as well. We won't get into these fixed, old patterns. It's a very big step."

"I have another question for Jeshua," I said. "What is the role and importance of sexual activity in older couples, including couples who have been together for a very long time, where maybe more thought and planning are needed?"

"Sometimes it's important to plan time and space for each other," he told us, "because when you've been together for a long time, you can kind of forget about yourself and the other person. It's important to keep the sense of freshness and wonder about each other, and it is possible.

"It's all about how the two souls relate to each other. As you become older, the sexual intimacy can gain a depth or dimension to it that is harder to attain when you're younger. Also, when you are younger and you have children, your attention gets caught up. You're very focused on everyday life, practical matters. It's like you are fully incarnated into the material world when you are raising a family.

"When you get older, you excarnate. Your focus on the material world becomes less. You're less fixated on goals for the future. So, there's more openness to the realm of the spiritual, and in your sexual life you can actually gain a sense of intimacy that is even more profound, that includes the physical but is less focused on the physical sensations. They are important, but it's more about tenderness and feeling completely at ease with each other.

Often this sense of intimacy can be there only if you've known each other for a long time. It's like the bodies become fluid in such an encounter. It's also a kind of mystical experience that you feel in such moments of intimacy. It can include the sexual act or having an orgasm, but it doesn't have to. It really doesn't matter so much. It's about the touching of each other to access a realm that is beyond the physical and that gives a great sense of warmth and comfort to both partners."

I then asked a question I knew was of particular interest to Sarah. "Jeshua, why is the 'chase' so important in sexual relationships? Usually, it's a man chasing a woman. Also, how can people move from the chase to an ongoing, intimate sexual relationship? In other words, a lot of times the man becomes less drawn to the woman because he 'has' her now that the chase is over."

"The whole idea of a man chasing a woman is not natural," Jeshua noted. "It's a construct. There is a belief or judgment that a man should perform sexually and therefore should chase a woman. Of course, there's a natural desire to want to connect with someone from the opposite sex, but it's actually as much present in a woman as in a man. But socially it has in the past been more acceptable for men to take the initiative. That's something very unnatural.

"What should happen when it comes to sexuality is that both girls and boys are raised to feel comfortable expressing themselves to each other. Then the notion of a chase will not be so evident anymore. When men believe that they have to perform or that it is an achievement to chase and to have a woman, then it's too much fixed on just this act. There's no real connection, and then the excitement disappears. When a man acts this way as a pattern, there's something else more complicated going on inside him, issues as to why it's hard to get into an intimate connection with a woman. You have to look at the individual to see what's really going on."

"In the case of Jim, this is a very big deal," Sarah shared. "He has been very focused on performing. For example, whenever we have been sexually intimate, he wanted to make me have an orgasm as many times as possible. This becomes oppressive. Our sensuality has sometimes gone past two hours. Why? It's that restrictive male role where they have to perform. We're not really connecting with each other. I'm trying to please him, and he's trying to please me, which is a very different thing."

"I feel that this need to achieve or to impress you is coming from a quite deep level of feeling not good enough, feeling insecure," Pamela told Sarah. Pamela was now using her clairsentience to feel the energy of Sarah and Jim's dynamic. "It's complex, because when you say you don't need to do that, then he could feel that as rejection."

"Yes, and does," Sarah confirmed.

"This is a good example of what men have been taught to do," Pamela added. "This is men not coming from their heart. Maybe women are more inclined to say, 'Let's let go of that achievement thing,' but for men it's not that easy because it's so much a part of their definition of masculinity. It's scary to let it all go."

"Jeshua," I asked, "when people are planning their lives at the soul level, and they're talking about entering into committed romantic relationships, how often is part of the discussion what their sex life will be like? And when they're planning to have little or no sex, is that usually planned as a possibility, a probability, or a certainty?"

"It's sometimes part of the soul's plan to have a marriage or intimate relationship that does not revolve around the physical so much," he told us. "Relationships often have one or two focal points or issues at the center. When two people meet on the soul level, they want to work or deal with certain issues, and sometimes the sexual is simply not so relevant. In that case sexual inactivity will not be an issue.

"There are, however, a lot of relationships in which the sexual dynamic is planned to be an important issue. It's important to look at the underlying dynamic, because when you say is it planned for a couple to not have a lot of sexual intimacy, if they're not having much sex, it's just an effect, but the underlying energy dynamics are the problem.

"So, there can be karmic issues between the partners, but karmic issues always point at general issues in someone's soul history. It could be, for example, that the soul wants to investigate or experience issues of abuse. There is actually a long list of issues related to the sexual problems in this area. If people experience sexual inactivity as a problem, then they need to look into it, and it's definitely part of the soul's plan to face it. This will raise a lot of things: old pain or judgment, what it's like to be a man or a woman. All these issues are touched; it's part of the soul's purpose. When you look at it from a higher level in this way, the collective consciousness becomes more free from the burdens of the past regarding sexuality. So, sexual problems are always related to the whole society. Sexuality is still very much tainted by the darkness, fear, abuse, and dogmas of the past."

"Is it only at the individual level that we can make change, or is there any way to make change on a societal level?" Sarah asked Jeshua.

"Women could play a leading role in opening the discussion about this," he answered. "Through their emancipation, women have become more independent, more in touch with their own lives, and have a natural understanding that sexuality is not just about physical gratification, desire, or lust. They have an innate understanding of the connection between the heart and the abdomen and of the spiritual role of sexuality, which is actually a sacred experience. It's important on a collective level to receive more information about and more understanding of the essential nature of the sexual encounter, and at this time women are more free to do this.

"Men are in a way still more haunted, more wounded by the traditional definitions of masculinity. They are a bit at a loss in this age. The old image of a man being strong, tough, and controlling—there's increasing criticism of that. So, men are told they need to connect with their sensitivity and feminine side; however, it's like coming out of a prison. It's not easy to do. In a way, women are in a better position to create a healing space for both themselves and men and also to inform society about other ways of dealing with intimacy and relating it to the whole human being."

"What is the role of pornography in this?" Sarah asked him, "because a lot of times when couples have sex, the man is using pornography. It's pretty common."

"In pornography there is an emphasis on achievement," Jeshua commented, "and there's a big lack of true intimacy and openness. When men are insecure but still have sexual desires, it can be an easy way out to watch pornography because it doesn't involve any need to open up. Insecure men could also think that's what's required of them: the achievement. Then they start to focus on that, and it creates a diminished or poor sense of what intimacy really means.

"This issue is closely related to how society raises and informs children: how you talk to them about sex. Often it is said to be an immoral or bad thing. How much room is there for a genuine, open conversation about the feelings teenagers have? They do not have information about what intimacy means. To really open that discussion would have a powerful effect on the minds of young men and women, boys and girls—and the appeal of pornography would end. Sexuality involving real intimacy, openness, and a sense of wonder and genuine connection is so much more fulfilling than pornography."

"The urge to watch pornography is a kind of escape," Pamela added. "It's painful for the person, if he's aware of it."

"I've always felt concerned about my husband's use of pornography," Sarah told us. "I've noticed that when we're closer, when we feel more intimate with each other, not physically even but just in general, he tends to use it less."

"Yes, because the intimacy fulfills a true need," Pamela confirmed.

∾

On the Earth plane, little is as it seems. Ostensibly, by the standards of modern culture, the celibacy in Sarah and Jim's relationship could be viewed by some as a failure, dysfunction, abnormality, or even lack of love. Yet, it was in pursuit of a higher understanding and eventual expression of love that Sarah and Jim planned the very celibacy that could be mistaken for love's absence. As Jim's soul told us, Jim is gaining clarity about what love is, and both Sarah and Jim are learning that deep love can be sustained without sex. The clarity and learning will in time allow them to infuse love fully into sexual form.

As souls, Sarah and Jim created a learning-through-opposites life plan. By experiencing the opposite of what they wish eventually to know, they come to understand better and value more greatly both sex and love. To undertake such a plan knowing it will cause temporary but significant suffering is an act of boldness. To live such a plan in a time period and society in which the divine purposes of celibacy are largely unknown is an act of extraordinary courage.

Just as contemporary society misjudges celibacy, so too does it miscomprehend vulnerability. The ability to self-defend is mistaken for strength; vulnerability is confused with weakness. In fact, precisely the opposite is true: defense is a form of attack, and great power lies in vulnerability. In search of these truths, Sarah and Jim have chosen celibacy as a path to complete openness, honesty, and vulnerability. When they attain those virtues, they will have mastered what Sarah's family called "the ultimate lesson": a self-valuing so profound that they can be in relationship with each other without fear. As they excise fear from their relationship, Sarah and Jim blaze an energetic pathway in which other couples may follow. Far from being some sort of failure, Sarah and Jim's celibacy catalyzes a personal and societal shift in romantic relationships. Such is the evolution: from love polluted and diluted by fear to only love.

When we create our pre-birth blueprints, we often plan to teach what we ourselves most need to learn. The lessons are intended for the teacher first. To the extent the teacher learns and lives those lessons, he or she becomes a more powerful teacher. Such is the path Sarah walks as she leads a class on women's empowerment in the company for which she works. Notably, the exercise she uses in her class is called The Courage Finder. The class in general and the exercise in particular are ways in which Sarah is learning to step into her own power and free herself from the collective feminine disempowerment of which Jeshua spoke. In this lifetime Sarah's soul wants her to come into a greater knowing of her own strength and power. Her soul's pre-birth intention is to cultivate certain virtues or knowings and then express them in some form of service to others. For Sarah, expression of feminine power in the class is cultivation of a knowing of that power. Here the twin intentions of cultivation and expression become one.

Importantly, part of Sarah's claiming of her feminine power is to be open about anger. If she is not, then her sexual energy goes *into* her anger. As Jeshua told us, Sarah's soul wants to be liberated from the old fears of self-expression (particularly as a woman) Sarah had in her past life with Jim. To the extent Sarah can be honest about anger with both herself and Jim, she will *release* the karma from the past life; that is, she will heal the underlying tendency that created the karma in the first place. She will also *balance* that karma by freeing sexual energy to be expressed sexually, rather than in anger, with Jim.

Sarah's cultivation and expression of her power allows her to move beyond our society's narrow, restrictive concepts of traditional gender roles. As Jeshua told us, over-identification with such roles will "limit your soul's expressive power." And just what is it our souls wish to express? It is connection, joy, and a celebration and sharing of one's uniqueness with one's partner. All these feelings can be expressed through sexuality, but none require it. Creative expression is sexual in nature and therefore serves as another form through which we as souls express ourselves. Even when the expression takes sexual form, "it doesn't matter to the soul whether you're in a homosexual or heterosexual relationship." For the soul, love is love in all its forms.

Speaking through author and medium Michelle McCann, a collective of angels has stated:

> "*Any circumstance* where an individual is not engaging in regular sexual activity was a pre-birth choice. The most common [reason] is that the soul wanted to know what it was like to live in a body and not experience sexual shame. Those souls choosing to live 'celibately' are healing the shame and pain of historical actions against others related to sex by living a simple and loving life without sex. There is nothing wrong with the person or people who make this choice. We would counter that in many ways they are more evolved souls as their pre-birth wish was to heal this part of themselves and the collective. *The most evolved souls live the life that makes them happy, regardless of what society and culture tell them they should do.*"

The angels, spirit guides, and other nonphysical beings who love us have no judgment whatsoever of anything we do or do not do. There is literally nothing anyone could ever do to be unworthy of love. Yet, on the level of the personality we harbor such strong judgments against both ourselves and others, including those who defy sexual norms. Like Sarah and Jim, those who choose not to follow socially accepted standards of behavior do so for both their own healing and that of the collective.

These are lives of heroic service.

Epilogue

EARTH IS THE MOST DIFFICULT planet in our universe on which to have an incarnation. After you have had a lifetime here, it becomes part of your energy signature, which consists of a combination of your unique color and your unique sound. It is through your energy signature that beings in the nonphysical realm recognize you. Names are not as important as they are here.

After this lifetime is over, as you travel throughout the universe doing whatever you choose to do next, other beings will see in your energy signature that you were on Earth. And their reaction will be something along the lines of "*You* went to Earth?? Wow!" That is, they are tremendously impressed! They know that it takes extraordinary courage to plan a lifetime on Earth and even more courage to execute the pre-birth plans once you are here.

I share this with you as a way of inviting you to be tremendously impressed with yourself. Respect and honor yourself for having the courage both to plan great challenges and to learn and heal from those challenges. That you are in a body on planet Earth automatically places you among the most courageous beings in the universe.

And regardless of whether or not you have had, currently have, or ever will have a romantic relationship in this lifetime, know this: You planned to cultivate profound, beautiful, wondrous, glorious love *for yourself.* This lifetime is the one in which hollow, meaningless notions like "unworthy" and "less than" are relegated to a spiritual dustbin. For millennia humans have looked without for what can truly be found only within. You came here to usher in an era of deep, much anticipated, long overdue self-love. You are the catalyst for the dawning of a planetwide recognition that each and every one of us is Divinity Incarnate.

You are the great love of your life.

Mediums and Channels

Barbara Brodsky
www.deepspring.org
bbrodsky@deepspring.org
(734) 477-5848 (Deep Spring Center)

Pamela Kribbe
www.jeshua.net
pamela@jeshua.net

Corbie Mitleid
https://corbiemitleid.com
corbie@corbiemitleid.com
(877) 321-CORBIE

Staci Wells
https://staciwells.com
info@staciwells.com

Printed in the USA
CPSIA information can be obtained
at www.ICGtesting.com
LVHW092136140923
758275LV00031B/225